The Author

JERRE MANGIONE was born of Sicilian immigrant parents who came to Rochester, New York, shortly after the turn of the century. He grew up among scores of relatives in a household where only Sicilian was spoken. Mr. Mangione worked his way through Syracuse University and later became an editor for a New York book publisher. In the 1940's, he served for six years as special assistant to the U.S. Commissioner of Immigration and Naturalization. Mr. Mangione is now professor of English and head of the creative writing program at the University of Pennsylvania. He is the author of six books, three of which deal with Italians.

America Is Also
ITALIAN

About the Book

This is the story of the 5,000,000 Italians who came to the United States to find a better way of life. The book explains why so many Italians left their homeland, the attitudes and ways of life they brought with them, and the impressive contributions they have made to the economy and culture of our nation. Captured are the drama, color, and fascinating qualities of the Italian Americans as they planted their roots deep into American soil and, along with their children and grandchildren, grew into an important segment of our population.

America is Also

ITALIAN

by Jerre Mangione

G. P. Putnam's Sons   New York

CONTENTS

For my Italian-American nephews and nieces:
Samuel James D'Amico, Roberta Kolp, Gap
Mangione, Charles Mangione, Josephine Shank,
Geraldine Williams, and Peter Morticelli

Other books by Jerre Mangione:

MOUNT ALLEGRO

REUNION IN SICILY

A PASSION FOR SICILIANS

THE SHIP AND THE FLAME

NIGHT SEARCH

LIFE SENTENCES FOR EVERYBODY

America Is Also
ITALIAN

1

The Italians Who Came Early

EVEN BEFORE the United States became a nation, a
number of Italians helped shape its history. First, of
course, there was Christopher Columbus. Without real-
izing it, he discovered a New World that was to become
the home of millions of immigrants from the Old World
of Europe. After him came several other daring navigators of Italian birth: John Cabot (Giovanni Caboto),
who with his son Sebastian discovered the coast of North
America; Amerigo Vespucci, whose first name became
the name of our continent; and Giovanni da Verrazano,
the first European to sail into New York Bay.

These are shining names in the pages of history. Less
remembered is a band of Italian Protestants known as
Waldensians, who in 1657 landed in the Dutch possession of New Amsterdam—the city that is now known

as New York. The Waldensians arrived less than forty years after the Pilgrims reached Massachusetts, and they came for the same reason the Pilgrims did: to live in a land where they would not suffer from religious persecution. In their own country these Italians were regarded as heretics. For more than two centuries Italian authorities had tried to force them to give up their religious beliefs, but without any success.

In 1655, when the Italian campaign against Waldensians became violent and a number of them were massacred, many of the survivors fled to Switzerland and Germany. Not all of them remained there, however. Some 200 Waldensians accepted an offer of the Dutch government to provide them with free transportation to New Amsterdam. Whether they remained there or moved on to Delaware, another Dutch possession, no one can say for certain. But the fact remains that New York City received its first Italian immigrants more than 150 years before our country became a nation.

Yet the Waldensians were not the first Italians to settle in this country. As early as 1610, only three years after the British founded Jamestown, Virginia, Italian craftsmen arrived there at the invitation of the British to teach their crafts to young apprentices. A dozen years later another group of Italians came to Virginia from their native Venice to set up a project for making glass beads that could be traded with the Indians. In the early 1700's still another group of Italians, experts in the field of raw silk production, traveled to the newly founded colony of Georgia, where they initiated a silk industry and taught others how to operate it.

Because of their superior skills as craftsmen, Italians were often invited to settle in the Colonies. The largest number went to Maryland, because it was a colony founded under Catholic auspices and most Italians were (as they still are) of the Catholic faith. But Colonial records show that Italians also settled in Pennsylvania, Rhode Island, and Connecticut.

More adventurous Italians became fur traders on the American frontier. Among them were the Tonti brothers, Enrico and Alfonso. In the course of expanding their trading activities with the Indians, they plunged into new territory that had never before been visited by white men. Enrico (also known as Henry de Tonty) is best remembered for his explorations of the Mississippi Valley. Alfonso became co-founder of Detroit and served as its governor for twelve years. His daughter was the first white child to be born in that city.

The wealthiest of all the fur traders on the Western frontier was Francesco Vigo, a big, burly Italian from Veneto. A staunch supporter of the American Revolution, Vigo served its cause as a solider, spy, and banker. At the risk of his life, he supplied valuable information to the American forces that helped them defeat the British in a crucial battle fought at Vincennes, Indiana. In his eagerness to see the American Army win, he spent his entire fortune providing arms and supplies. After the war the Americans expressed their gratitude to Vigo by making him a citizen of the new nation, by naming a county and township after him, and by perpetuating his memory with a life-size statue that was erected in the city of Vincennes.

Another Italian name closely linked with the American Revolution was that of Captain Richard Talliaferro, the descendant of an Italian who had settled in Virginia in 1635. Captain Talliaferro fought so bravely that a monument in his honor was built on the spot where he was killed in battle. But the Italian name that is most closely identified with the ideals of the American Revolution is not that of a soldier; rather it is that of a political philosopher. Filippo Mazzei, a native of Florence whose democratic views had forced him into exile, had long promoted the principle that all people have the right to live their own lives without being oppressed by any government.

At the invitation of Benjamin Franklin, Mazzei came to Virginia from England in 1773 for the purpose of conducting agricultural experiments. But his close friendship with Franklin and Thomas Jefferson soon led him to become involved in the American struggle for independence. Using the pen name Furioso, Mazzei wrote a series of articles for the *Virginia Gazette* which attacked the British for their misrule of the American Colonies and urged an independent form of government that would provide equality for all men. The articles, written in Italian and translated into English by Jefferson, had a strong influence on the thinking of Americans who were to become the leaders of the Revolution that followed.

In one of his articles Mazzei wrote: "All men are by nature equally free and independent . . . equal to each other in natural rights." Jefferson was so impressed by this thought that when he wrote the Declaration of Independence, he was inspired to translate it into the immortal phrase "All men are created free and equal."

Mazzei's forcefully expressed views probably hastened the Colonies' break with England. He was able to convince some of the American statesmen that total independence was necessary. Although the Italian philosopher had no official part in the establishment of the new nation, one writer has noted that he could well be considered an "assistant Founding Father." Jefferson must have had a similar opinion, for in one of his letters he referred to Mazzei's "early and zealous cooperation with the establishment of our independence."

The great-grandson of one of the early Italian settlers in Maryland did play an official role in the founding of the United States. He was William Paca, a member of the Maryland legislature and the Continental Congress. He was one of the signers of the Declaration of Independence, and later became governor of Maryland.

The Italians who came to the United States between the Revolution and the Civil War were relatively few in number, estimated at about 12,000. Their impact on the nation, however, was considerable. Unlike the mass of Italian immigrants who were to start coming toward the end of the century, these Italians were mainly from the North of Italy, and a fairly high percentage of them were educated men, who quickly found places in American society as doctors, lawyers, teachers, and ministers.

Educated or not, they were an enterprising lot. Willing to go anywhere in their search for economic opportunities, they scattered to all parts of the country. Some 300 of them traveled across the continent during the California gold rush of 1849. Few found gold, but many remained to become fishermen or to cultivate vineyards that eventually led to the establishment of California's thriving wine industry.

An outstanding Italian immigrant of that era was Francesco Vigo's nephew, Paolo Busti, who arrived in 1850 as the American agent for the Holland Land Company. The company owned about 5,000,000 acres of undeveloped land in New York and Pennsylvania. Busti, an experienced land developer, transformed this vast wilderness into sites for villages, towns, and cities. Buffalo, some historians claim, was one of the cities.

In that same period G. P. Morosini, an Italian who had arrived in the country as a penniless sailor, also helped stimulate economic progress. He became an influential banker, a partner of the renowned railroad magnate Jay Gould. There was also the Italian American Giuseppe Tagliabue, who invented and manufactured valuable instruments for navigators and meteorologists, and Louis Tinelli, who pioneered in American silk.

Some of the poorest Italian immigrants became America's earliest missionaries of popular culture. They were the Italians who went from street to street selling statuary or playing music. The first artworks of any kind owned by thousands of American families were the statuettes of historical and mythological figures peddled by these immigrants. The earliest musical performances heard by Americans were often those of the Italian strolling musicians.

In later years the street musicians included hundreds of picturesque organ grinders, who cranked out a steady stream of Italian arias. Each organ grinder usually traveled with a companion—a saucy monkey on a leash. The monkey would hold out his cap for coins after each performance and then delight audiences with his comic bowing and scraping whenever anyone gave money.

Because the nation was so new and a great deal of physical energy was required to build its economy, Americans had little time to encourage an appreciation for good music. The encouragement at first came largely from Italians who had been accomplished musicians in their homeland. For example, it was Filippo Traetta, an Italian composer, who founded the first American conservatory of music in Boston in 1803 and later founded a second conservatory in Philadelphia.

The Italian immigrant who dominated the American musical scene in those years was Lorenzo da Ponte. When he arrived in New York at the age of fifty-six, he was already famous as a libretto writer for the most famous of Mozart's operas. Da Ponte had been an adventurer with a somewhat dubious past (an ex-priest who fled to America to shake off his London creditors), but he soon became highly respected here for his successful activity in making Americans more appreciative of Italian opera.

Da Ponte established the New York Opera Company, the first serious attempt to present opera regularly in the United States. A brilliant impresario, writer, and scholar, he became identified with Italian culture in general, so much so that in 1825 Columbia College (not yet a university) appointed Da Ponte its first professor of Italian language and literature.

Italy was not yet a nation during this period. It was made up of a series of states, like Piedmont and Sicily, which had separate governments that were under foreign domination. Although there had been several attempts by Italian patriots to free the states and unify them into one nation, they had not proved successful. The Italians who took part in these attempts were considered dangerous radicals by the authorities and had to find refuge outside their homeland.

A large group of these exiles chose to come to the United States because our country was recognized the world over as a haven for all men who believed in freedom and democracy. In New York they organized an "Italian Guard" for the purpose of training soldiers who would one day fight for Italian unity and independence. But before that day arrived the American Civil War broke out, and many members of the "Italian Guard" joined the Northern Army to help preserve the Union. They fought bravely in all the great battles, and three of them were singled out for their unusual courage and given the nation's highest military award, the Congressional Medal of Honor.

Among the Italian exiles to arrive here before the Civil War was the famous Italian general and hero Giuseppe Garibaldi, who later was to liberate the Italian people from their foreign rulers and make it possible for them to achieve unification. While Garibaldi waited for a strategic time to resume his military campaign in Italy, he lived in the home of an Italian inventor friend, Antonio Meucci, in Rosebank, Staten Island, and earned his livelihood working in Meucci's candle factory.

Abraham Lincoln was one of Garibaldi's warmest admirers. After Garibaldi had scored a series of military triumphs in Italy that removed the chief obstacles to unification, President Lincoln offered him the post of major general in the Union forces. "Tell him," he wrote his American representative in Europe, "that this government believes he will, if possible, accept this call, because it is too certain that the fall of the American Union . . . would be a disastrous blow to the cause of Human Freedom, equally here, in Europe, and throughout the world. . . . General Garibaldi will recognize in me not merely an organ of the government, but an old and sincere friend."

Although Garibaldi replied that he would be "happy to serve a country for which I have so much affection and of which I am an adoptive citizen," his countrymen would not permit him to accept President Lincoln's offer. They insisted that he remain in Italy to lead a march on Rome, which was still under foreign rule.

The birth of the Italian nation was finally achieved in 1871, but it created many new and painful economic problems, particularly for the people in Southern Italy, where the economy was largely agricultural. Heavy taxes, overpopulation, and insufficient land made it difficult for most Southern Italians to earn decent livelihoods. They began to look for work in other parts of the world, especially in France and in North and South America.

At first the Italian immigrants favored such countries as Brazil and Argentina, which were then in their earliest stages of development. But in the 1880's an increasing number of them began to come to the United States.

By the beginning of the twentieth century millions of Italians were pouring into New York Harbor, setting in motion what has been called "modern history's greatest and most sustained movement of population from a single country." By 1925 the Italian immigrants were to number more than 5,000,000, and they had become the second-largest foreign-born group in American history.

The largest of all the immigrant groups was that from Germany. German immigration reached its peak in 1882 and eventually totaled almost 7,000,000 persons. The Irish formed the third-largest group. Like the Germans, they began coming shortly after the founding of our nation. As economic conditions in Ireland grew worse, Irish immigration to America increased. By the time the Civil War began there were more than 1,500,000 Irish immigrants in the country. In the ensuing years their number more than tripled.

At first most Americans were in favor of admitting large groups of immigrants. The general attitude was that ours was a land for all people who were economically or politically oppressed. It was also agreed that a nation as young as the United States could use all kinds of workers, skilled and unskilled, and it did not matter what part of the world they came from. There was such a desperate need for workers during the Civil War that President Lincoln proposed setting up a system for "the encouragement of immigration." He was thinking not only of the present, but also of the future. He realized, as did other American statesmen of that era, that if the United States were to fulfill its tremendous economic potential, it must have a much larger population.

Not all Americans shared this point of view. As early as the 1850's "America for Americans" became the slogan of the Know-Nothing Party. Its supporters maintained that most immigrants were paupers and criminals who would surely destroy the country. Since they represented a small fraction of the population, the Know-Nothings made little or no headway. But in 1883, when the country suffered an economic depression that was to continue for three years, anti-immigration sentiment spread quickly. More and more native-born workers began to blame bad times on the foreigners' willingness to work for low wages.

In their fear that immigrants would take away their jobs, native Americans revived the slogan "America for Americans" and in every possible way expressed their hostility toward foreign workers, particularly those of the Catholic faith. Some of them joined such organizations as the Ku Klux Klan and the American Protective Association, which seriously claimed that Catholic immigrants were trying to place the control of the nation in the hands of the Pope.

As the antagonism toward immigrants grew, several states enacted laws that barred aliens from state and municipal jobs. In Congress there were several attempts to pass laws that would restrict immigration, but they were not successful then. The anger toward the immigrants reached a pitch of violence in several parts of the nation. In the coalfields of Pennsylvania a group of Italian and Hungarian workers, who had been brought there as strikebreakers (unknown to them), were attacked by armed American coal miners. Several of the immigrants were killed.

One of the most shocking acts of violence against immigrants took place in New Orleans in 1891 shortly after the city's superintendent of police had been murdered by unknown persons. In the hysteria that followed the crime, suspicion fell on the Italians in the city (most of them were Sicilians), and a number of them were placed under arrest. But there was no intention of giving the arrested Italians a fair trial. Before the trial opened, the mayor of the city announced: "We must teach these people a lesson they will not forget for all time."

Although the court failed to find any of the Italians guilty of the murder, a mob of 5,000, led by some of New Orleans' leading citizens, stormed the jail without any interference from the police and killed 11 of the jailed men. Afterward a spokesman for the mob blamed the massacre on the jury that had acquitted the Italians. "The people demanded that these murderers be punished with death," he said. "We have executed their will."

A little later it was discovered that eight of the murdered men were naturalized Americans; three were citizens of Italy.

The episode, a disgrace to the principles of justice, scandalized the whole world. The Italian government withdrew its minister from Washington and broke diplomatic relations with the United States. Not until the following year, when the American government paid $25,000 to the families of the three non-American victims, were relations resumed.

Despite the wide publicity given to this grisly affair, Italians and other immigrants continued to come to the United States in increasing numbers. Instead of coming from Germany, Ireland, and the Scandinavian countries, as had the majority during most of the nineteenth century, the largest numbers were now coming from the Eastern and Southern nations of Europe—from Russia, Austria-Hungary, Poland, Greece, and Italy. They kept coming for more than a quarter of a century until the doors to America were almost entirely shut.

2

The Flight to Ellis Island

POVERTY WAS the many-headed monster that drove millions of Italians out of their native land. "When I found that the only way I could prevent my family from starving was to turn to stealing, I decided it was time to go." That is how my great-uncle explained why he and his family left their village in Sicily and traveled to America at the turn of this century.

Poverty has never ceased to be a brutal force in the lives of Southern Italians. In that particular era its brutality was clearer than ever. Italy had become a unified nation with a democratic constitution, but the South had not reaped any economic benefits from this development. Conditions had, in fact, worsened, for although nothing had been done to stimulate the stagnant economy of the South, new taxes had been imposed on its people.

By and large, the South still retained its feudal character. Most of the land remained in the hands of a few wealthy nobles, who lived in the North and left the management of their huge estates to an exploiting class of leaseholders known in Sicily as *gabelotti*. Interested only in quick profits, the *gabelotti* were unconcerned about the welfare of the land and of the peasants. They took advantage of the peasants' desperate need for work by offering them sharecropper terms that were grossly unfair. The land fared no better. It was not irrigated, no trees were planted to stop erosion and floods, and little was done to improve the quality of the soil. As the land grew poorer, so did the peasants.

Conditions were better in the North of Italy, where new industries were being established. But the same government policies which helped the North prosper placed a staggering tax burden on the people of the agricultural South. They paid taxes not only to the national government and the provinces but also to their local communities. One of these taxes, the so-called family tax, was especially unpopular. Its purpose was to tax every family for everything it owned, but rich families were sometimes allowed exemptions that were not allowed to the poor. A peasant, for example, would be taxed for the horse he needed to do his farmwork, but a rich man would be exempted from paying a tax on the horse he rode for sport.

There were other factors that made the situation of Southern Italians intolerable. One of them was malaria, a disease that killed thousands of Southern Italians and left many more ill the rest of their lives. The disease was particularly devastating in Sicily. There the failure to replace the forests that had once covered this beautiful island created swamplands and pools which became the breeding grounds of mosquitoes carrying deadly malaria germs. To lessen the danger of becoming infected, the peasants began building their homes on hilltops away from the swamplands, and this meant another financial burden for them.

The lot of the peasants was also made more desperate by two other unfortunate developments. In 1890 a plant parasite known as the phylloxera destroyed most of the grapevines in the Italian South. As a result, Italy dropped to second place in the export of wine (France jumped to first place, where it has since remained), and thousands of farmers suddenly found themselves without a means of earning a livelihood. The second tragic development in Southern Italy was the cholera epidemic of 1897, which claimed many lives and spurred thousands of Italians into leaving the country.

The Italian peasant was not the only one who suffered from the general poverty of the South. Skilled workers, such as my great-uncle who was a blacksmith and my cousins who were stonemasons, were also badly affected. Of the 2,300,000 Italians who migrated to the United States during the height of their exodus, between 1899 and 1910, about 15 percent were men with skilled occupations; nearly all the others were farmworkers or laborers. The great majority of these immigrants came from the South of Italy; only 400,000 were Northern Italians.

Two-thirds of the Italian immigrants during that period were men. Many of them expected to stay in the United States only long enough to earn enough money to improve their family situation in Italy. Others left with the hope of sending for their families later on. In a country like Italy, where the family unit is stronger than in most other countries, it was an emotional strain for husbands and brothers to part from their close relatives and go to a land which had a different language and strange customs. But like most of my own relatives, they had no choice in the matter. They had to go where they could earn money, and from all indications, the United States seemed like a paradise for all who were willing to work.

To bolster their courage and their hopes, they listened eagerly to the propaganda of steamship company agents, who tried to drum up passenger trade by telling the Italians about the opportunities and wealth that awaited them in the United States. And they read and reread the letters that came from relatives already in America, who often offered to send money for their passage and promised to help them find jobs. What finally clinched the decision of many an Italian to join the migration to the United States was the rumor that the American government might soon tighten its immigration laws and reject all those without special skills and education.

Among poor Italians, education was considered a luxury which only the rich could afford. Almost every male child was expected to help support his family as soon as possible. Children born in a peasant family seldom saw the inside of a schoolroom. As soon as they could do any work, they helped with the farming. The less fortunate children went to work in sulfur mines. The luckiest ones were those apprenticed to artisans and thus able to learn a trade. Education was considered a waste of time for girls; at an early age they were taken out of school to help with the housework or embroider. It is little wonder that more than half the Southern Italians who arrived in the early years of the century could neither read nor write.

Many of the Italians who decided to come here had never been out of their hometown. For them the journey to the United States was an exciting but worrisome adventure. American laws had reduced the hardships of ship travel known to earlier immigrants. But the ships were still overcrowded and badly ventilated, and the food was so bad that many of the passengers could not eat it without becoming ill. The immigrants usually traveled in steerage because it was cheapest. Even the peasants who had been living in dire poverty found it a grueling experience.

Describing the conditions on ships bearing immigrants, an American government report said in part:

The ventilation is almost always inadequate and the air soon becomes foul. . . . The reek of food and the awful stench of nearby toilet rooms make the atmosphere of steerage such that it is a marvel human flesh can endure it. Most immigrants lie in their berths for most of the voyage, in a stupor caused by the foul air. . . . All of these conditions are naturally aggravated by overcrowding.

On the subject of overcrowding an Italian immigrant, who had embarked at Naples with his sister, recalled that he never saw his sister during the voyage because "people in different compartments went on deck at different times and then had to go back to make room for the others." The same immigrant said that sleep was difficult on the ship because a horse belonging to a first-class passenger had been placed among the people in steerage. "He was a nervous horse, and he stomped a lot and neighed and made other noises that kept us awake."

Another immigrant remembered that everyone slept in his clothes, with his luggage on the mattress because there was no other place for it. He added that the passengers ate in their bunks. "We each had a plate and a cup and a spoon. The cooks came with big pots of soup and stew and filled our dishes, but most people did not even try to eat. We had to wash our things and ourselves in salt water. Many of the passengers got skin infections and split lips from the dried salt."

But physical discomfort was only part of the anguish that the immigrant experienced during his journey. There was the sadness of having parted with one's family and village, and above all, there was the general fear that the American authorities might refuse to let him enter the country. Whether an immigrant ship was headed for New York, Boston, or Philadelphia, there were always frightening stories exchanged about immigrants who, for reasons that remained a mystery, had been ordered to return to their homelands.

Not all the passengers were steeped in gloom. Some

of the Italians tried to cheer their companions by playing mandolins and guitars, and sometimes there was dancing. For the first time in their lives Italians from different parts of Italy found themselves mixing with one another. There were Neapolitans and Sicilians and Italians from the provinces of Abruzzi, Apulia, Basilicata, Calabria, as well as those from northern provinces. They each spoke a different dialect, and sometimes the Southern and Northern Italians could not understand each other.

Then, as now, these two groups of Italians had mixed feelings about each other. The Northerners tended to look down on the Southerners because of their lack of education. The Southerners, on the other hand, were inclined to consider the Northerners snobs. Yet as the ship approached the land of their hopes, the attitudes softened, and occasionally, before port was reached, lifelong friendships would develop between them.

In New York, where most of the immigrants landed, the steerage passengers were taken in barges to that world-famous immigration station Ellis Island, where they received a medical examination and were questioned to determine whether they met the requirements of the American immigration laws. The name "Ellis Island" often struck terror in the hearts of the immigrants, for it was there that they would learn whether or not they could enter the country.

Recalling what Ellis Island was like at the turn of the century, Frank Martocci, who had been an American immigration inspector for many years, said that the steerage passengers who were immigrants would be lined up with their identification tags on them—"a motley crowd in colorful costumes, all ill at ease and wondering what was to happen to them. Doctors then put them through their medical inspection. Whenever a case aroused any suspicion, the alien was set aside from the others, put in a cage like a segregated animal, and his coat was marked with a colored chalk. The color of the chalk showed why he had been separated from the others. . . . "

The rest of the immigrants were asked such questions as: "Where in the United States are you going? By whom was your passage paid? Is that person in the United States or not?" The questions were asked to make certain that the immigrant had friends or relatives in America who would look after him until he could support himself. Another reason for asking the questions was to determine whether or not the immigrant was coming to the United States as a contract laborer. A law passed in 1885 made it illegal for an American employer to promise an alien that he would give him a job on his arrival or pay for his passage. The law had been passed because too many American employers who had lured immigrants here by such promises had then taken advantage of them by insisting on long periods of employment at unfair wages and poor working conditions.

The questions asked by the immigration inspectors alarmed many of the immigrants. Not knowing what the requirements of the law were, they were afraid of saying the wrong things by mistake and being sent back. Although there were always interpreters present to make the questions understandable, there was no time to explain the laws fully.

One of the interpreters was Fiorello H. LaGuardia, the

son of Italian parents, who later became one of New York's greatest mayors. He worked at Ellis Island as a young man from 1908 through 1910. "I never managed during the years I worked there," he wrote in his autobiography, "to become callous to the mental anguish, the disappointment and the despair I witnessed almost every day. . . . At best the work was an ordeal."

Ordinarily, the medical inspection and questioning would take about an hour, and the immigrant would then be free to leave Ellis Island for New York. But always there were immigrants who would be detained on the island until their cases could be examined more carefully. They were kept in quarters that were often more crowded than those in steerage. Food was just as poor as, and sometimes worse than, that on shipboard. At one time the immigrants were served nothing but prunes and prune sandwiches. "It was a case of profiteering," according to Frank Martocci. "The man in charge of the food was making money out of the poor devils by giving them the cheapest food he could find."

The story of Ellis Island is filled with tragedies. Thousands of immigrants took their lives because they could not bear the strain of waiting to learn if they would be permitted to enter the country. There was also the tragedy of families being separated and of women with children waiting in vain for their husbands to claim them. Sometimes the husbands had either died or had disappeared, and the women and children would be returned to their native lands.

A number of young immigrants tried to escape from Ellis Island by swimming ashore, but nearly all of them failed. A large percentage of those detained on the island did not meet the immigration requirements and had to be sent back to their own countries. There were at least 1,000 such cases each month; often there were ten times that number. A good many of them, of course, were Italians.

One of them was my Aunt Teresa, who was anxious to join her husband in Rochester, New York. Twice she was obliged to return to Italy because the medical examiners decided she had trachoma, an infectious disease of the eye. On her second trip to Ellis Island, her passport was not in order, and she was kept there for eight days. "It was like a prison," she once told me. "I spent all my time looking through barred windows at the skyline of New York and crying."

A determined woman, my aunt made a third and successful effort to be admitted. This time she came by way of France, where she charmed the medical examiners into believing that nothing could be seriously wrong with eyes as beautiful as hers. She also took the precaution of traveling second class and in that way avoided the medical inspection at Ellis Island that was given to all immigrants who traveled in steerage.

Once the immigrants set foot in the United States, they had an urgent financial problem because they had brought little or no money with them. A study of the Italians arriving in 1910, for example, showed that the average sum of money among them amounted to only $10. However, most of the immigrants who were going beyond New York City already had railroad tickets to places where they expected to find jobs quickly through relatives or friends who had arrived before them.

The immigrants willingly went to all sections of the country where there was a demand for workers. Most of them settled in cities. There was hardly a city of any size that did not soon have a Little Italy in its midst, big neighborhoods of immigrants who usually came from the same Italian towns and villages. The largest of all the Little Italys was in New York City, for it was there that thousands of Italians expected to find the most job opportunities. There, too, they could be certain of encountering so many other Italians that they would soon feel at home.

The United States was then in a period of vast industrial expansion. There was a tremendous demand for unskilled labor, and the immigrants had no trouble finding work. If relatives or friends could not help them get jobs, there were employment agents who could, with railroad companies, iron and coal mines, steel mills, and factories of all kinds. The Italians hired by such agents found themselves traveling much greater distances than they had anticipated—to states as far as Nebraska, Montana, Washington, Oregon, and California. But since their chief purpose in coming to America was to find employment, they did not mind.

In his absorbing book *Immigrant's Return,* my friend Angelo Pellegrini tells of his father who had come to the United States alone and who wound up 7,000 miles away from his family in McCleary, Washington, as an employee of the Northern Pacific Railway. The father had arrived in 1912 with the idea of working for three years and then returning to Italy with what he had saved. But within a year he was convinced that the Northwest was a good place to rear his family and sent for his wife and five young children.

Angelo Pellegrini, who was then nine years old, remembers the journey from Genoa to New York as a nightmare, chiefly because of the frightening rumors that were circulated on board the ship. One rumor claimed that one of the passengers had been stricken with a rare and contagious disease, and for that reason, the American authorities were not going to permit anyone to land. Another frequent rumor was that the United States had become so jammed with immigrants that there was no more room for anyone else. But the worst nightmare of all, it turned out, was trying to find the father.

No one in New York seemed to know where McCleary, Washington, was. It could not be found on any map or train schedule. The immigration authorities finally put the mother and children on a train headed for a city in Washington, hoping that someone there could direct them to McCleary. The family, who had no idea how far Washington was, had expected to be with their father within a few hours. But they traveled for seven days, with not enough to eat because they could not make themselves understood.

Arriving at the place marked on their tickets, they were shocked to find that Father Pellegrini was not there to meet them. They were further horrified when the Americans in the railroad station insisted there was no such town as McCleary. "Tired, hungry, desperate, convinced that the whole journey had been a malignant hoax," writes Angelo Pellegrini in his book, "we children burst into tears."

Then suddenly a little man appeared in the station and spoke to them in Italian, a language they had not heard from others since their departure from New York. "Why are you crying?" were his first words. Miraculously, he turned out to be a friend of their father who knew exactly where the tiny town of McCleary was located, 200 miles farther west, and he undertook to take them there himself.

At last, after a journey that had taken almost a month, the family found their father.

3

The Troubles They Knew

THE MAJORITY of the Italians in the mass migration
that began toward the close of last century were farmers.
Yet once they arrived here, few of them chose to earn
their livelihood off the land.

There were a number of reasons for this sharp break
with their past. One was that they were obliged to earn
money as quickly as possible. Farming requires capital
for the purchase of land and equipment, and they had
none. Moreover, by the time they arrived here it was too
late to obtain free land or buy it cheaply, as earlier immigrants had done. For a period following the Civil War,
the American government had virtually given every immigrant interested in homesteading a 160-acre farm.
But this practice had ended by the time the Italians
came. They were the first immigrants to arrive in this

country in large numbers who could not have easy access to land.

There were also psychological reasons why so many Italians turned their backs on farming. For one thing, their bitter experiences on the land in Italy led them to associate farming with all the horrors of poverty. Another reason was that the American farmer's way of life did not appeal to them. American farmers lived in comparative isolation, with few neighbors. The Italians, on the other hand, were used to living closely together in villages, from which they made daily trips to the lands they tilled. They had no wish to live apart from one another.

But it was more than the dread of loneliness that suddenly changed the Italian peasant into an American city dweller. It was also the uneasiness of finding himself in a foreign country where most people did not speak his language or understand his needs and habits. To ward off despair, he had to be among his own kind, even though it often meant living in dark and dirty city tenements. Only in that way could he solve the problem of communication and feel reasonably safe.

The new immigrant had a fear of being cheated by Americans, and in his mind, almost anyone who did not speak Italian was an "American." As soon as he arrived, his countrymen warned him not to trust "Americans." One of the first words they taught him was "ghirarahir," which was supposed to mean "get out of here." He was urged to yell that word at any American who approached him.

There were many stories he heard to deepen his distrust of Americans. One of them, told by my Uncle Nino, dealt with the experience of the first group of Italian workers to come to Rochester, New York. The people of that city made it amply clear to them from the start that they were not welcome. They refused to sell the Italians food, nor would they rent them houses, hoping that the immigrants would become discouraged and leave. For a while the Italians lived in boxes and tents and ate nothing but whatever dandelion greens they could find. When they could no longer endure this situation, they decided it was time for a showdown.

Arming themselves with the pickaxes they used in their jobs as laborers, the Italians marched into one of the largest grocery stores in the city. By the use of sign language they threatened to tear the place apart unless they were permitted to buy the food they needed. The clerks hastily sold them all they wanted. Later, when the weather turned cold and snowy, they marched into the same grocery store with their pickaxes, this time to demand that houses be rented to them. The grocery clerks interpreted their demand to the police, and the police explained the problem to the town council, which ordered the landlords to stop discriminating against the immigrants. Within a few days the Italians were able to move out of their boxes and tents into warm houses.

In all American cities where they went, the Italians tried to live among those who spoke the dialect of their native region and observed the same customs. They hardly ever had any dealings with non-Italians, except for the men they met on their jobs and the Irish- and German-American priests they heard in church. They would have preferred listening to priests who spoke their language (there were not enough Italian priests in those days), but they did not mind the foreign-sounding priests since they represented God.

Through their children the Italians were sometimes surprised to learn that the angry English words they occasionally heard from the pulpit were not part of a sermon dealing with sin and damnation but a scolding for not giving the church more money to help pay its coal bill. It was a new experience for the Italians to contribute for a church coal bill, but gradually it was one of the American customs they learned to accept.

At first they resisted any changes and tried to live as they had in Italy. They shopped at stores run by Italians. They went to Italian lawyers, doctors, dentists, shoe-makers, and barbers. Nearly all their business and social life was conducted in their native tongue. This was especially true of the Italian women, who hardly ever encountered Americans. Even when the women worked in factories, as thousands of them did, they were likely to be surrounded by other Italians. It took the women a longer time than the men to lose their fear of the New World.

The immigrants had many fears. In some families, like mine, parents became so afraid of losing communication with their American-born children that they would not permit English to be spoken in the home. As a result, many Italian parents lost a fine opportunity to learn English from their children. And the children, in turn, often learned an inferior brand of Italian at home, a local dialect which only a few Italians could understand. The immigrants would, of course, have found life in America far easier had they been able to learn English soon after their arrival. Some did. But after a long day's work, most of them did not have the energy to study the language in night school.

The immigrants' general lack of English made them dependent on the few Italians who knew the language and could act as interpreters. Unfortunately, not all these interpreters were honest. Some took advantage of the immigrants' ignorance of America. They overcharged them or took money from them for services which they could not deliver. More often than he realized, the immigrant who thought he would be treated more fairly by an Italian than by an *Americano* was cheated.

The unfriendly attitude of the American press toward the Italian immigrants convinced them that they must remain separate from the American world around them. As more Italians kept pouring into the country— as many as 15,000 in a single day—more newspapers reflected the anti-immigration feelings of their readers. One newspaper went so far as to call the arriving Italians "a horde of steerage slime." Such words of hate served to spread even more prejudice against the immigrants.

Curiously enough, the sharpest antagonism toward the Italians was often found among men and women who themselves were immigrants, the Irish and the Germans in particular. They helped popularize such contemptuous names as "wop" and "dago" for the Italians.

Later on, many of their children were to intermarry with the children of the Italian immigrants, but in those times they were far from friendly.

In the South there was such contempt for the Italians that it was claimed that because of their swarthy complexions, they were not members of the white race. One employer was quoted as saying: "It makes no difference to me whom I employ—Negro, Italian, or white man." The Southerners often resented the Italians because of their insistence on treating Negroes as their equals. In a small Louisiana town five Sicilian storekeepers, who had become friends with some of the local Negroes, so enraged the townspeople that they picked a quarrel with one of them over a goat, then lynched all five of them.

In other parts of the South, Italian children were forbidden by law to attend white schools. And in South Carolina a state law prevented the Italians from migrating there.

One of the unfair impressions of the Italians spread by newspapers in all parts of the country was that they were generally a criminal lot who carried stilettos and belonged to some secret criminal organization, such as the Mafia and the Black Hand. Many Americans, especially social workers and teachers, protested that most Italians were honest persons who never broke the law. They pointed to a study which showed that crimes by Italian immigrants were of a lower percentage than crimes committed by native-born Americans. But the press disregarded all this and continued their anti-Italian campaign.

The word "Mafia" was especially prominent in its headlines and created a great deal of confusion in the public mind about the nature of that criminal organization. In Sicily, Mafia gangs had developed during many centúries of foreign rule when the population was badly exploited. Gradually, the Mafia gangs became the private armies of the fedual lords and, by means of terror and violence, imposed their own code of law and order on the people—a code that forbade, on penalty of death, any cooperation with police authorities.

Despite the attempts of the Italian government to prevent its criminals from leaving the country, a few managed to enter the United States at the height of Italian emigration. Singly and in groups they operated in a number of American cities, where most of their victims were Italians. During the late twenties their criminal activity grew much stronger as they were joined by some second-generation Italian Americans who, after a slum childhood, turned to crime. Using Mafia tactics, the new and old criminals organized themselves into various racketeering gangs that preyed on all American society. Although their number was tiny, the sensational publicity they received had a harmful effect on the good name of the Italian-American population.

At one point in 1908 the Sicilians of Rochester, New York, felt obliged to convince the rest of the community that although there were a few among them who had committed crimes, they were mostly a law-abiding and civilized people. These Southern Italians were proud of their ancient culture, with its Greek, Roman, and Byzantine heritage. Even though they had had little schooling, they wanted the American community to know that they were worthy of respect.

From this desire grew the idea of staging the Passion play, a drama about the life of Jesus Christ which has a large cast of characters and numerous scenes. More than a score of Sicilian workers banded together for this purpose. Milkmen, shoemakers, bakers, tailors, factory hands, and ditchdiggers became the actors of the drama. After their day's work and on Sundays these men and women met for a series of rehearsals that went on for months. The undertaking grew. Hundreds of other Italians in the city pitched in to make the sets and costumes and contributed toward the expenses of the production. Their earnings were small, but they gave all they could spare.

The group also had the help and encouragement of one American — a social worker named Florence Kitchelt Cross. On the eve of the production she explained in one of the Rochester newspapers that "the Italians are sensitive to criticism and are very much hurt by the actions of a few of them. . . . They have decided to produce 'The Passion Play,' not to make money, but to show that they have a great reverence and respect for holy things."

October 12, the day celebrating Columbus' discovery of America, was the date chosen for the production, perhaps in the hope that on that day the Americans would "discover" the good qualities of the Italians in their midst. But, alas, except for a few Irish policemen and the social worker, there were no Americans in the audience. Nevertheless, the play went on, and it was a beautiful performance, which everyone in the auditorium wildly applauded. The excitement it generated continued after the curtain came down and spread through the city with lightning speed.

Encouraged by the enthusiastic reception, the players decided to put on a second performance. This time the theater was packed with both Americans and Italians. Although the lines spoken were in Italian, the Americans were deeply moved by the production. The next day the same newspapers that had been featuring Italian crime on their front pages devoted the same space to praising the quality of the production and thanking the Italian community for making so impressive a contribution to the cultural life of the city.

But it takes more than a play to change public opinion. Within a year, the newspapers were back to their old custom of giving an undue amount of space to any crime committed by an Italian. Disappointed that the dividends of winning community approval had lasted such a short time, the Italians sadly retreated into their own world again.

Actually, Italian immigrants throughout the country had more serious problems on their minds than that of trying to improve their public image. Working conditions were often unhealthful, wages were too low, and jobs were unsteady. When business was down, factory workers would be sent home for weeks at a time, without pay. The Italians with construction jobs were no better off; they found that there usually was no work to be had during the winter months.

Their American-born children provided the Italians with one of their chief worries. It often seemed to them that some of the values they carefully taught their children at home would be canceled out by what the children learned from their American playmates and teachers. They were convinced, for example, that American schools failed to teach children the importance of respecting parents. The Italian fathers were especially bitter and concerned about this point.

In Italy it went without saying that a father could expect his children to honor and obey him in every particular. But here an Italian father often had trouble imposing his wishes on his children, especially if the wishes were at odds with American custom. For this reason there was often a great deal of friction between parents and children.

Much of the friction was caused by the American custom of allowing boys and girls to date. Here it often happened that youngsters went out together for an evening without having a chaperon along. In Southern Italy such a thing was unheard of, and if it happened, it would have created a scandal. Only young men and women who were engaged to be married were allowed to be together, and even then they had to be chaperoned.

Some Italian fathers also objected to the American custom of letting young men and women decide for themselves whom they would marry. Marriages in Italy were often arranged by parents, without considering whether the young man and woman loved each other. The American custom of divorce caused even greater alarm among Italian parents. In Italy there was no divorce. Because there were so many divorces in this country, the immigrants decided that Americans could not possibly make good husbands or wives and did everything they could to persuade their children to marry only persons of Italian ancestry.

Some of the fears the Italians had for their children were justified. Occasionally their children slipped completely away from their control, joined a juvenile gang, and got in trouble with the police. This happened most often in New York, Chicago, Philadelphia, and Baltimore, where thousands of Italian immigrants were jammed together in slum neighborhoods that had been deeply encrusted with dirt long before they got there. New York, which had the most immigrants, had the worst slums —tenements five and six stories high honeycombed with tiny, airless rooms, with as many as a half dozen persons living in each room.

There was rarely any sunlight. The rows of tenements were like tall mountain cliffs that blotted out the light. Often the buildings were on streets with elevated trains, and the soot from them frustrated the immigrants' most valiant attempts to keep their rooms clean. In the summertime the Italians tried to escape the suffocating heat of their quarters and spent as much time as possible outdoors. The streets and sidewalks were so constantly crowded that the children had nowhere to play.

In such a congested and squalid atmosphere it was difficult for the parents to keep track of what their children were doing. Although they did their best to find out, often it was not until a policeman appeared at their door that they learned their children had broken the law. The miracle was that more children of Italian immigrants did not get into trouble.

More than 1,000,000 of the immigrants who arrived

early in the century became dissatisfied with life in the United States and returned to Italy. They left for a variety of reasons. Some were disappointed that America had not turned out to be the moneyed paradise they had expected. Some became ill from working in cold climates to which they were not accustomed. Some became discouraged by their failure to obtain steady work. Some had saved a bit of money and thought they could now lead an easier life in Italy, where the cost of living was lower.

There were some who returned to look for an Italian wife. Others were simply homesick or could no longer bear the pain of living away from close relatives. There were also those who became bitter over the anti-immigrant sentiment in America and were convinced that our nation had lost its standing as "the land of the free." The largest exodus of Italians took place between the years 1908 and 1916. After that the pattern began to change.

By 1920 there was a sharp decrease in the number of "birds of passage," as returning immigrants were called. The millions of Italians in the country became aware there would be no turning back; they would make the United States their permanent home. Despite all the hardships of living here, they realized that their future and that of their children were brighter in the United States than they could be in Italy. One indication of their faith in their American future was that in 1917, 30 percent of all the schoolchildren in New York City were found to be of Italian parentage.

Although many of the immigrants remained in neighborhoods where they had first taken up residence—Italians are by nature a people who like to stay put—thousands of families were able to move away from slum tenements into homes with backyards. There they could breathe more easily and plant a garden—even a fig tree to remind them of their native land. The fig tree had to be carefully wrapped in rags each year to protect it from harsh American winters. But the Italians never minded this chore, for the memory of their homeland would always remain dear to them.

4

The Way They Lived

WHEREVER THEY settled in America, the Italians tried to be as near one another as possible. They were by nature a gregarious people. D. H. Lawrence, the British novelist who once lived in Sicily, observed that the Italians there "hang together in clusters and can never be physically near enough." In their New World, where the immigrants' need to be together was even stronger than it had been in their homeland, the Italians spent most of their free time in a long round of social gatherings with friends and relatives.

At least once a week, usually on Sundays, as many families as could be crowded around a dinner table would pass a good part of the day together. The occasion would start with a dinner of many courses (the immigrants did not believe in stinting on food, especially when there was company) and be followed by the men's favorite card game, *briscola* or *scopa*. While they played, argued, and drank red wine, the women would sit nearby sewing and gossiping, and the children would chase one another in an endless game of tag. The more children there were, the better everyone liked it, for children were the immigrants' greatest love.

Amid all the shouting and noise, a phonograph would blare out the soulful words of an Italian opera, usually the work of the composer they esteemed above all others, Giuseppe Verdi. No matter how many rooms there were in the house, all the social activity would take place in one room. The guests would usually remain until midnight. They hated to say good-bye, and sometimes later in the night they would return with mandolins and guitars to serenade their hosts with Italian love songs and folk tunes.

There were always parties of one kind or another, not only for birthdays, anniversaries, and important saints' days, but also when a child was baptized, when he received his first communion, when he was christened, and when he was graduated from school. The arrival of new immigrants was always a good excuse for another party, as was the opening of a new barrel of wine. Grandest of all were the wedding parties. These often took place in an enormous hall, so as to crowd in as many friends, acquaintances, and relatives as possible, and the feasting and the dancing would last far into the night, long after the bridal couple had left for their honeymoon.

Everyone danced at weddings, young and old, for everyone knew how. As soon as a child was old enough to walk, his mother would start teaching him her favorite dances —the waltz, polka, and the mazurka. When the child was older, he might learn the tarantella, a fast, whirling Italian dance which was named after a poisonous spider whose bite was said to make its victims move about wildly.

Although the Italians were constantly surrounded by friends, they were always eager to make new ones. The more friends an immigrant had, the more secure he felt. Often, he would go outside his family group to become friends with someone he had met at work or at a party. To make the friendship official, the Italian would ask his new friend to be the godfather of his newborn child and in that way become his and his wife's *compare*. The wife of the friend would become their *comare*. After that they would treat each other like the closest of blood relatives.

The Italians formed close friendships not only for social reasons but also to help one another. No matter what repairs an Italian needed in his home, there was always some relative or *compare* who would happily take care of them without charge. A skilled plasterer, carpenter, or plumber would spend a great deal of his spare time working for his friends. In turn, he could always depend on their services. Even if they were not skilled workers, they could always help him dig a cellar, plant a vegetable garden, or make wine.

Few of the immigrants had ever made their own wine in Italy. But when American Prohibition was enacted and it was no longer legal to buy wine, the Italians took lessons from friends who were experts in winemaking and began to produce their own. Although they drank moderately, they could not imagine eating a meal without drinking wine. It was part of their daily fare, and they even encouraged their children to drink wine in the belief that it was good for them.

After a few lessons from the experts, Italians like my father began to take considerable pride in the quality of the wine they made. Great care was taken to make certain that the proper kinds of grapes were bought (the grapes usually came from California, where they were often grown by other Italian immigrants) and that the kegs were properly aged. After the grapes were mashed and their juice poured in the kegs, there would be an impatient time of waiting and testing. Sometimes the final result was vinegar, and an expert would be hastily consulted to find out what had gone wrong. But often no one was consulted for fear that news of the failure would become widely known and the winemaker would become the butt of many jokes.

The Italians who had some land around their houses also took pride in their gardens. Many an immigrant family raised tomatoes in the backyard and flowers in the front. The tomatoes were used to make fresh spaghetti sauce, and if there were enough of them, they would be canned for use in the winter months. Some of the tomatoes were mashed and dried in the sun to make a thick tomato paste which the Italians called *stratto*. It, too, was saved for the winter.

The unhappiest of the Italian immigrants were those who lived in big-city tenements, farthest removed from nature. But although they could not grow any of their own food, they kept on preparing the same dishes they had known in Italy. As a result, a number of Italian immigrants began to operate groceries or pushcarts to sell their compatriots the foods they could not find in American stores. Large, open-air Italian markets, with scores of pushcarts, became part of the scene in every Little Italy in the nation. There the immigrant housewives and often the men themselves (in Southern Italy the shopping is nearly always done by the men) would bargain with the vendors for greens, olive oil, black and green olives, cheese, macaroni, and seafood of all kinds—sea urchins, mussels, devilfish, squid, and razor clams. In every market place there were merchants who shouted or sang out their wares in the dialects of their native villages. Listening to them and seeing the vast display of Italian foods and breads (sometimes placed next to pushcarts featuring underwear and socks), the immigrant customers found it easy to imagine that they were in the heart of Palermo or Naples.

Of all the foods, bread was considered the most precious by all Southern Italians. It symbolized the blessings of life, and also all the hardships their ancestors had endured through the centuries to keep body and soul together. When times were especially bad, they told one another, "As long as God gives us a piece of bread, we shall get along." And when a male child was born in a peasant family, he was regarded as "a gift from God with a loaf of bread under each arm."

Because bread represented something holy to the immigrants, they paid careful attention to its treatment. It was considered a sin, for example, to place a loaf of bread on a table wrong side up, or to play with it, or to throw any of it away. They also took great pains making it as attractive and as tasty as they knew how. Some of the loaves had flower designs on them. Some were shaped like a woman's braids. Others were round and sprinkled with sesame seeds. The most popular design, both with housewives and professional bakers, was a round loaf with three gashes on top of it—a warning to the devil of what might happen to him if he came where he was not wanted.

Most of the immigrants who lacked education brought their superstitions with them, ancient beliefs that had been developed through centuries of fear. Above everything else, they were afraid of the "evil eye." There were agents of the devil everywhere, they believed, ready to make you ill or bring you bad luck just by looking into your eyes. Some of these agents were said to be persons of good intentions but who had been selected at birth by the devil to do his dirty work, and there was nothing they could do about it. To protect themselves against the "evil eye," the superstitious carried amulets around their necks which could break any evil spell. As a further protection, they placed a pair of bull horns over their doorways, so that no one could bring any evil spirit into their homes.

There were a number of minor superstitions which most immigrants, educated or not, accepted. If a fork dropped from the table, my mother would know that someone was gossiping about her or about some other member of her family. If a knife fell, she could be certain that someone was about to call. Spilled olive oil was considered a bad omen unless one quickly sprinkled salt over it. Yet to spill wine was said to bring good luck— especially, as my father liked to point out, if there was enough left in the bottle for another round.

Dreams were taken seriously because it was believed that they forecast the future of the dreamer. If a person dreamed of marriage, for example, he could expect a death in his family. But if he dreamed of death, it meant that he would go on enjoying good health.

Although their superstitions were mainly based on fear, their religious customs were born of hope. They were usually happy occasions. Their celebrations in honor of the Virgin Mary and of their favorite saints became an important part of the immigrants' social life. As soon as Little Italys began to form throughout America, the people in them began to stage the same religious festivals they had known in their native towns and villages.

Putting on a *festa* was an expensive undertaking, for it meant hiring a band, buying hundreds of street decorations, and paying for the elaborate fireworks display that usually climaxed the ceremonies. Although their salaries were small, the Italians cheerfully contributed whatever the *festa* cost. For them the annual celebration for a cherished saint was the most exciting event of the year. It banished the drabness of their surroundings for a while, and it gave them the hope that the saint they were honoring might someday use his or her powers to make life easier for them.

One of the most popular festivals was that of San Gennaro held annually in the Mulberry Street section of New York City, one of the country's most populated Little Italys. There every September the Neapolitans celebrated the birthday of their patron saint with a round of festivities that attracted both Americans and Italians from all parts of the city.

In the same month the Sicilians who lived in the same Little Italy held their annual *festa* for the patron saint of Palermo, Santa Rosalia, who was said to have sacrificed her life to stop a severe epidemic that was killing off many Palermitans. Every February another group of Sicilians paid homage to Sant'Agata for saving the city of Catania from certain destruction during an eruption of Mount Etna. According to legend, the flow of molten lava from the volcano had reached the very edge of the city when Sant'Agata intervened and miraculously changed its direction with her veil.

In almost every American city where there were Italian immigrants there were likely to be annual religious festivals. One of the most elaborate was the one in Omaha, Nebraska, where for several days the Italians honored Santa Lucia, the fourth-century martyr who was said to have cut out her eyes because their beauty had attracted a nobleman who was a heathen.

The statue of Santa Lucia, a life-size figure with a small stiletto piercing the neck, was the center of the celebration. Nearly every day the statue was paraded from street to street, on one day in a huge flower-decked float pulled by a team of devout Italians. During each procession the immigrants pinned dollar bills on the saint's robes or dropped coins into Italian and American flags that were held stretched out between the paraders.

Some of the women brought their babies, disrobed them, and gave the clothes to the saint as an expression of their gratitude for keeping their children in good health.

The Italians had great faith in the power of saints to help them during illness. They attributed different kinds of healing powers to different saints. If a person were bitten by a dog, for example, he and his family would address their prayers to St. Vito. And if the trouble was with the eyes, then Santa Lucia was the saint to receive the appeal.

Too often, the immigrants had more faith in their saints and the Madonna than they had in doctors and hospitals. For a long time they were suspicious of doctors whose language was foreign to them, and many were afraid that going to a hospital meant certain death.

Whenever this or any other tragedy befell the immigrant, they usually placed the blame on *destino*—fate— for, like their ancestors, many of them believed that everyone's life is mapped out in advance, and there is nothing anyone can do to change that which *destino* has planned. In a country as poor as Southern Italy, life was stagnant, and people did not know the meaning of change. They assumed that a man's life, from the time he was born to the time he died, had to remain more or less the same. No wonder that they believed so strongly in destiny.

Not until the Italians had lived in the United States did they begin to understand that it is possible for men and women to change their lives. Despite all their harsh difficulties in the New World, they began to see that life need not be static here; change is nearly always possible.

The immigrants gradually began speaking less of *destino*
and for the first time dared dream of a life with a brighter
future. The awareness came slowly, as many good things
do, but it was probably the most valuable contribution
that America made toward the happiness of the Italian
immigrant.

Once an immigrant had succeeded in bringing his
family here, his first hope for the future was to own a
house and be free of landlords. Houses in America were
usually larger and more expensive than houses in Italy,
and he and his family had to work hard in order to save
enough money to make the down payment that would
give them ownership. Buying a house often meant going
into debt for many years, but the Italians were not discouraged. The satisfaction of owning their own homes,
especially one with a yard for gardening, outweighed all
other considerations.

Yet the immigrants as a rule did not take on debts
lightly. Although American merchants were at first re-
luctant to allow them credit, they soon found that the
Italians were among the most reliable customers they
had. The immigrants had a strong sense of responsibility
and felt bad when any one of them did not fulfill his
obligations. Sometimes they tried to make amends for
such persons. One of my father's *compari* recalls that
when he lived in a New Jersey town early in the century,
an Italian woman moved away without paying the bills
she owed to a local department store. When the other
Italians heard about it, they took up a collection and
paid her debt so as to keep their reputation in the community "free of stain."

Conscientious though they were in the payment of their bills, most immigrants were constantly in debt no matter how many members of the family had jobs. There was seldom enough money for any luxuries. Yet there was one luxury they could not resist—opera. For the first time in their lives they were able to indulge in their passion for their favorite form of entertainment. Until they came to America, most immigrants had heard opera but had seldom seen it performed. Here they could attend all the operas they loved. At every opera performance in every American city they packed the galleries (few could afford seats anywhere else in the auditorium) and with hands, throat, and feet expressed their joy and appreciation for what was happening on stage. Their applause made all other applause in the auditorium sound feeble.

Once an immigrant family acquired a house, it often went further into debt and bought on the installment plan a player piano, as well as a phonograph. With the phonograph the family could hear the recordings of Enrico Caruso, the famous tenor, and other favorite opera stars. The player piano, which was especially popular with Italian immigrants in the twenties before the advent of radio, served a twofold purpose. By simply pumping the instrument, they could hear piano renditions of any music they liked and follow the words of the music printed on the piano roll. The player piano could also be used to provide the children in the family with music lessons—a luxury that would have been out of the question with poor families in Italy.

Many an immigrant mother would scrimp to save

nickels and dimes out of her weekly food allowance so that her children might have the services of a piano teacher at least once a week. The children did not always respond to the lessons, for some of them did not share their parents' enthusiasm for music. But the mothers persevered in their efforts, each staunchly believing that each of her children was a potential concert artist.

Italian parents were willing to provide piano and violin lessons for their daughters, as well as their sons. But when it came to deciding how much schooling their children should have, they generally favored the sons. Like their Old World ancestors, they saw little point in keeping their daughters in school for any longer period than the law prescribed. A daughter, they felt, had but one goal in life: to be married and have a family. In Italy she would have been kept at home to sew and cook until she was married. Here, where girls enjoyed more freedom, the parents allowed each daughter to take a job in a factory or a store until the right man came along to marry her.

Their attitude toward their sons was quite different, especially as they came to realize that anyone in America, regardless of how poor his parents were, could achieve a high standing in the community if he received enough education. Their fondest dream was to have at least one son become a doctor or a lawyer. Among Italians these had always been the most respected professions; the medical profession was rated above all others. It was said that if the son of an Italian immigrant could stand the sight of blood, then the parents would hope that he could become a doctor; otherwise, they hoped he would train to be a lawyer.

But not many immigrant families could afford to pay for all the years of education these professions required. Some of the sons, who could not become doctors, became pharmacists or dentists. And in some instances the sons who could not afford to attend law school became teachers. Many others were not as fortunate, for the majority of immigrants were not able to send their children past high school. They had to console themselves with the hope that perhaps their grandchildren would one day receive as much education as they wished.

5

The Work They Did

"NEVER BEFORE," wrote Albert Q. Maisel in his 1948 book *They All Chose America,* "had so large a group stepped so quickly into the mainstream of American life. In the span of a single generation millions of Italian Americans have come to occupy a position of full equality —and often of great distinction—in every field of endeavor."

How the Italian immigrants accomplished this miracle is one of the great success stories in history. When they first began arriving in great numbers during the nineties, they had nothing but their willingness to work. Except for a few who were educated or who were trained artisans, the only jobs they could find were those that called for unskilled labor and paid the lowest wages. Their poor standard of living was made even poorer by their obligation to save enough money to send for their families in Italy.

In the nineties their sad condition prompted the United States Commissioner of Labor to report that in the nation's four largest cities about one-third of all the Italian immigrants there were living in a state of desperate poverty. The impression given by the report was that these immigrants seemed incapable of bettering their situation. What it failed to take into account were the qualities in the average immigrant's character that were to make him a valuable member of American society: his courage, his industry, and his strong sense of family responsibility.

The Italians came with high hopes, convinced that this was the land of opportunity and grateful for the chance to work. They took whatever jobs were offered to them, even though the working conditions were sometimes unhealthful and dangerous. Often, they were badly exploited by their employers, but they kept on working. Throughout the closing years of the last century and the early decades of the present one, they supplied the muscle which helped to build America into the richest nation in the world.

During America's busiest years of industrial expansion, they did a great deal of its hardest work. They built railroads that linked the nation more closely together. They dug out canals and paved roadways for transporting goods. They made reservoirs and dams for generating electric power. They mined for coal and iron and manned the steel furnaces. They were in the phosphate mines of the South, the silver mines of the West, and the stone quarries of New England. They took jobs in textile factories, silk mills, and the big garment industry. They worked as hod carriers, mortar mixers, plasterers, bricklayers, and masons, and they constructed factories, aqueducts, office buildings, and houses. Wherever there was hard work to be done, the Italian immigrants were almost certain to be there.

Like all immigrants of that era who were employed as unskilled laborers, they sometimes had horrible experiences. For example, during the 1914 strike in Ludlow, Colorado, seven young Italian children and a woman were burned to death when state militiamen set fire to the tents where the Italian coal miners made their homes. On that same grim occasion, the militiamen also shot to death three of the miners. But the most frequent tragedies were those inside the coal mines. Before unions had become powerful enough to insist on safety precautions for miners, coal mine operators did little to protect their lives, and scores of workers were buried alive in cave-ins.

Recently the son of an Italian immigrant told me about his father whose first job in America was in a Pennsylvania coal mine. Accustomed to working as a farmer, the father hated the darkness of the mine, but it was the only place where he could find employment. One morning he refused to go to work, explaining to his family that during the night he had dreamed the mine collapsed and killed most of the miners. A superstitious man, the father was certain that the dream was a portent of what would happen. When two weeks had passed and there had been no mishap, he decided to ignore the dream and return to work. Within a few hours he was in the midst of an explosion that killed several of his fellow workers and fractured his skull. "It was the last time he ever went down in any mine," his son told me. "As soon as he was well, we moved to Buffalo, and he got an outdoor job as a ditchdigger."

The railroad workers were among the most exploited of all the Italian immigrants. In their travels around the country laying down tracks or doing maintenance work, they often slept in windowless boxcars, on mattresses seething with roaches and bedbugs. Rain or not, they were expected to work at least ten hours a day. Their miserable conditions were often imposed on them by other Italians—the *padroni,* which is the Italian word for "bosses." The *padrone* not only bossed the immigrant railroad workers but also acted as their agent. Because the immigrants spoke no English, they often had to rely on a *padrone* to find them jobs and make all necessary arrangements with the employers. The *padrone* charged the Italians a high fee for their services and profited from their inexperience in every other possible way.

For example, if an immigrant had to travel to another city to start work on a new job, the *padrone* who took care of his transportation would charge him the cost of a first-class railroad ticket, even though he traveled by coach. And when, as often happened, there was a delay between one job and another, the *padrone* would install the immigrant in an expensive boardinghouse and share the profits with its owner. There were also many instances when a *padrone* would persuade an immigrant to quit his job so that he could collect a commission for finding him another.

The average salary for a railroad worker was $10 a week, but the immigrant seldom got a full week's pay. His pay envelope first went to the *padrone,* who subtracted from it whatever money was owing to him for the immigrant's food. "I kept a list of the boss' food prices and the regular store prices at one city in Ohio," recalled an Italian who was part of a railroad work gang, "and always the prices charged by the boss were two or three hundred percent higher."

In the first decade of this century the average weekly earnings of an Italian worker varied from $9 to $11 a week, while those of a native worker were almost $14 a week. But even though the Italians worked for less pay, they could not be sure of working every week. The average annual earnings of an Italian immigrant amounted to less than $600. A native worker earned twice as much. Not until the Italians began joining unions and demanding higher pay and better working conditions did their situation improve.

The subway workers in New York City were the first of the Italian immigrants to band together into a union. The American historian who wrote that "the greatest metropolis in the world rose from the sweat and misery of Italian immigrant labor" may have had them partly in mind. So much "sweat and misery" were demanded of the men who did subway work that the Irish and Polish laborers, who were among the first to take such jobs, refused to go on working in the subways. The Italian immigrants willingly took their places, and at the beginning of the century some 4,000 of them were burrowing their way into Manhattan's rock and soil to build the Lexington Avenue subway.

Although the Italians worked swiftly and well, their employers treated them even worse than they had the Irish and Polish workers. Conditions became so intolerable that the men in self-defense formed a union led by a twenty-one-year-old Italian, Salvatore Ninfo, who spoke some English. The workers soon went on strike and won their demands for higher wages, shorter hours, and safer working conditions. Four years later, in 1904, another group of 5,000 Italian workers, who were building the Bronx Aqueduct, went on strike and also won all their demands.

One of the most radical changes in the life of the arriving Italian family was that for the first time Southern Italian wives and daughters went to work in factories. In their homeland it was considered improper for any woman to work anywhere but in her home. In many parts of Sicily, for example, the women were not even allowed to help with the farmwork. But here this ancient feudal attitude was at once replaced by the American attitude that there is nothing wrong with a woman taking a job. Soon after the mass arrival of the immigrants, the factories of the nation were filled with Italian women employees of all ages.

They worked mostly in textile and garment factories under miserable conditions. The worst of the tailor factories became known as sweatshops, and the men who operated them were called cockroach bosses because of the vermin that infested their factories. Many of the factories were dangerous firetraps, and nearly always the machines used by the workers lacked any safety features. Eventually, thanks to such militant labor leaders as Luigi Antonini and Augusto Bellanca, the workers were able to insist on improved conditions.

The tailor factories attracted the greatest number of Italian women employees. The garment industry in Philadelphia became almost entirely made up of Italian women and men. In New York, Chicago, and Boston the Italians numbered one-third of all the garment industry employees.

Italian workers and Italian labor leaders played a key role in one of the most dramatic strikes in American labor history—the 1912 strike of textileworkers in Lawrence, Massachusetts. More than 300 strikers were arrested on charges ranging from riot to murder. The strike was led by a Socialist poet, Arturo Giovannitti, and two other Italians. When one of the workers, Anna Lo Pezzi, was shot and killed during a clash between the police and strikers, the three strike leaders were arrested on charges of murder. At their trial they were found innocent, but throughout the strike the men were kept in jail.

One of the strike's most publicized highlights was the Exodus of the Children. Inasmuch as the children of strikers were not getting enough to eat, scores of them were sent to New York City, where they were taken in by families who sympathized with the workers' cause. The first group of children to arrive from Lawrence by train was greeted at the station by large and cheering crowds.

The strikers won, but their victory was a small one—a

wage increase of one cent an hour. The Congressional investigation that followed revealed that many of the employees in the textile mills were children in their earliest teens and that families were living in wooden firetraps, "dark and damp" rooms that bred disease. It was also found that most of the workers were not eating well enough and suffered from malnutrition.

A year later there was another famous strike that involved a large number of Italian workers—this time in the silk mills of Paterson, New Jersey. One of the immigrant strike leaders was Carlo Tresca, an eloquent giant of a man who later was to become New York's leading Italian anti-Fascist. Although the Paterson strike was one of the longest in that city's history, the workers lost it.

Unfortunately for the general welfare of the Italian immigrants, the great majority of them were slow to appreciate the advantages of belonging to unions. By nature, they were a basically conservative people, wary of any group activity. In fact, "He who plays alone always wins" is one of the Sicilians' favorite mottoes. Since most of the immigrants came from an agricultural economy where unions were virtually unknown in those days, they tended to be suspicious of all American unions at first, not understanding how much they might benefit from joining them.

The Italian newspapers they read did little to enlighten them. Many of them were published by men with right-wing attitudes, who were opposed to unions during the very years when the immigrant workers had most need of them. The most influential of these newspapers was the daily *Il Progresso Italo-Americano,* which is still published. *Il Progresso,* as it is commonly known, was founded by a former *padrone,* Carlo Borsatti. Later its publisher became Generoso Pope, an Italian immigrant who made a fortune in the sand, gravel, and contracting business.

Despite all handicaps, the Italian immigrants who survived the early brutal years of adjustment somehow managed, through their talent for work and for learning, to acquire skills and to raise their standards of living. By 1930 the number of unskilled Italian workers in New York had declined to the point where only 10 out of 100 men had jobs as laborers. The longer they remained in America, the more enterprising many Italians became. A great number of them set up grocery stores and meat markets, fruit and flower stands, restaurants, shoeshine and beauty parlors, shoe repair and barber shops, tailoring establishments, storage and moving facilities.

They also flourished as fashion designers, cabinetmakers, hairdressers, chefs, machinists, plumbers, electricians, mechanics, painters, paperhangers, and carpenters. Some of the same laborers who had earned their livelihood with pick and shovel became prosperous construction contractors equipped with steam shovels, pneumatic drills, and fleets of trucks. And some of the poorest of the immigrants achieved executive posts in the fields of merchandising, manufacturing, and banking.

Although the number of Italian immigrants who took up farming was relatively small (about 10 percent), they became the chief suppliers of fruits and vegetables for many an American city. They were particularly successful in the field of truck farming. A typical success story is that of Italian farmers around New Haven, Connecticut, where the Italians formed the city's largest group of immigrants. Speaking of their achievements, former President William H. Taft in 1921 praised the Italian farmers for taking land that was going to waste and gradually transforming it "into productive gardens, magnificent vineyards, fields and orchards rich in fruits and vegetables" which supplied New Haven and created "a new source of wealth beyond the fondest expectations of anyone."

As early as 1880, a colony of 6,000 Italian peasants at Vineland, New Jersey, had demonstrated what superb farmers they could be when they had enough land and incentive. Both were provided through the farsighted thinking of an Italian, Secchi de Casale, and the co-operation of a generous American landowner, Charles Landis. A fighter for Italian independence, De Casale had become interested in the problems of the Italian immigrant while living in New York as a political exile. He was one of the first to recognize that immigrants who had been peasants in Italy would be happier and more prosperous in this country if they could work as farmers. Landis agreed with him and placed at his disposal large tracts of land around Vineland for De Casale's colonization plan. Within three years after their arrival, the Italian peasants had cleared the land and made it prosper. At first they cultivated vineyards and produced wine. Later they branched into the more profitable occupation of truck farming, specializing in sweet potatoes and other vegetables that were in demand in nearby cities.

A number of the early Italian farming colonies in America were made up of former railroad workers who, in their travels, found land that appealed to them and settled on it as farmers. One such colony was established in Bryan, Texas, by 350 Sicilians who had been working for a railroad company. When the men found that the Americans didn't want the land along the Brazos River because it was flooded every spring, they bought it for little money and sent for their wives and children. Working together, they turned the land into thriving cornfields and cotton plantations. As they prospered, the settlement grew into a town with fifteen stores and a church. At first, when there was no school, the Sicilians sent their children to the nearest school, 10 miles away, on muleback and in donkey carts.

There were similar colonies in Louisiana, Alabama, North Carolina, Arkansas, Missouri, New York, and Wisconsin. In almost every instance, there were battles to be fought with nature before the land could be made productive. There were also times when the Italian farmers had to battle against the hostility of neighbors. One such battle happened in Arkansas to a colony of Italian farmers at Tontitown, named after the Italian-American explorer Enrico Tonti.

In addition to such natural disasters as a cyclone and a drought that ruined all their crops, the Tontitown colonists were beset by a mob of their American neighbors who burned down their schoolhouse. When the Italians refused to be frightened away, the mob returned to destroy their church but were stopped at its door by an Italian priest armed with a gun. Yet Tontitown eventually became a prosperous farming community, and even won the favor of most of its native-born neighbors.

The Italian farmers who went to California, along with the Italians in the East who became truck farmers, were among the most successful of all. California had a special appeal for the Italians because much of it resembles their homeland in climate and soil. As early as 1904 a government report noted that there was hardly a single California valley where there were not a dozen or more Italian farms, orchards, and vineyards. The orchards often bore olives, oranges, and lemons—the same products that are prevalent in Sicily. A number of the Italian vineyards grew to become a basic part of California's rich wine industry.

Fishing was another occupation that naturally attracted large numbers of immigrants from Southern Italy. Many of them settled in New England, particularly around Boston and Gloucester. Others traveled as far west as California. Fisherman's Wharf in San Francisco is probably the most famous of all the Italian-American fishing settlements. It was there that one of the great ballplayers of all times was born—Joe DiMaggio, whose parents had migrated from a small Sicilian fishing village near Palermo.

Wherever the immigrant fishermen went, they worked for wages at first, but within a few years many of them owned their own boats and some became owners of large fishing fleets. At Fisherman's Wharf a number of the immigrants formed a cooperative during the thirties and named it the Crab Fisherman's Protective Association. The group owned its boats and equipment in common, and all profits were equally divided among the members of the association.

Cooperatives were then unknown in Southern Italy, where every fisherman worked for a *padrone* or for himself. That these Italian Americans could achieve such a democratic arrangement meant that they were learning to trust one another in the country of their adoption as they had rarely been able to do in their native land.

Knowingly and often unknowingly, the mass of Italian immigrants was adjusting to the American way of life.

USA

6

The Wars They Fought

The Uprooted is the name of a book about American immigrants that was written by the son of Russian immigrant parents, Oscar Handlin. His title is an apt description of how the immigrants felt when they first arrived in the United States. Because all human beings have a need to feel rooted to the place where they live, the immigrants worked hard to plant new roots in the country of their adoption. They accomplished this by helping build America with their labor and by doing the best they could for the future of their American-born children. "To have American-born children," an Italian immigrant father once told me, "is to become an American for the rest of your life."

But while the Italians and the other recent immigrant groups were trying to nourish their new roots, powerful forces were at work to prevent other immigrants from coming to the United States. There were many complaints about the immigrants who were already here. The loudest one was that they were "too foreign" for this country and could never become "good Americans." The complainers ignored the fact that ever since the birth of the American nation, and even before it, nearly all its people had consisted of immigrants and their descendants.

One of the nation's leaders who favored restrictions that would reduce immigration sharply was Senator Henry Cabot Lodge. Ever since 1891, Lodge had been trying to enact a law that would deny admission to immigrants who could not read or write. Three times the literacy test bill he sponsored had been passed by Congress, and three times it had been vetoed by a succession of Presidents—Grover Cleveland, William Howard Taft, and Woodrow Wilson. With every veto the White House reminded Congress and the American people that a literacy test was contrary to the spirit of the nation's democratic tradition. But in 1917 Congress passed the bill over President Wilson's veto, and it became the law of the land.

The literacy test became the first big step taken toward stopping the heavy flow of immigration from such impoverished European nations as Italy, Greece, and Poland, where any schooling was beyond the means of most poor families. An unknown poet expressed the unhappy reaction of some of the immigrants to the new law:

> We've dug your million ditches,
> We've built your endless roads,
> We've fetched your wood and water,
> And bent beneath your loads.
> We've done the lowly labor
> Despised by your own breed—
> And now you won't admit us
> Because we cannot read.

The literacy test had hardly gone into effect when the United States entered World War I, and all immigration was sharply reduced until the end of the war. As soon as the American declaration of war was announced, a large contingent of Italian immigrants left the country to do military service in Italy, which was one of our allies in that war. But the great majority of Italian immigrants remained and vigorously supported the war effort of their adopted country on the domestic and the military front.

About 12 percent of the American Army was made up of Italian immigrants and their American-born sons. They gave an impressive accounting of themselves. The American government awarded 100 of them Distinguished Service Crosses. Of this number, 83 were American soldiers who had been born in Italy.

Among the war's most outstanding heroes were two sons of Italians, Private Michael Valente and Private Joseph Mastine. Both received Congressional Medals of Honor. After the war, the Department of War pointed out that although the Italians constituted 4 percent of the nation's population, the list of war casualties showed that a full 10 percent of the men had Italian names. In the same year, the Provost Marshall praised all the foreign-born residents of the nation for proving themselves loyal during the war. "No need to speculate how it came about," he wrote, "the great fact is demonstrated that America makes Americans."

But the excellent war record of the American immigrants did not prevent the rise of anti-immigration sentiment. The literacy test was not enough for those who wanted "America for the Americans." Now they began to demand new immigration laws that would keep the country "more American." During this period, a book by Madison Grant entitled *The Passing of the Great Race,* which attacked the recent immigrant groups as a weak and inferior people, became the bible of those who wanted to see immigration stopped or further curtailed.

Madison Grant was a racist who held that persons from Northern Europe were superior to those from the Mediterranean and Balkan nations. He referred to immigrants who were not "Nordics" as "human flotsam" and insisted that they had lowered "the whole tone of American life." Nowadays most Americans would consider Grant's views highly absurd, but at the time they were taken seriously by a number of prominent Americans. A dozen years after Grant published his book, the same views were expressed by one Adolf Hitler, whose belief in the superiority of "Nordics" led to the destruction of 6,000,000 European Jews.

As soon as World War I ended, many Americans began to fear that despite the literacy test, millions of Europeans from Southern and Eastern Europe would try to enter the country, and their clamor for further immigration restrictions became louder and more general. Some of it stemmed from influential labor leaders, who feared that the admission of more foreign-born workers would create a cheap labor market, which would lower wages and cause general unemployment. Like other opponents of immigration, they chose to ignore the economists who could prove that the United States had experienced its greatest periods of prosperity during the very years when immigration was at its height.

One of the chief charges against immigrants was that too many of them were radicals with dangerous "foreign" ideas. Although most of the leading radicals of the period were native-born Americans, the "foreign radicals" were held largely responsible for the nation's labor disturbances. This general attitude was officially aided and abetted by the Department of Justice. In 1919 it arrested and deported many aliens on the grounds that they were dangerous radicals who were responsible for a great deal of subversive activity throughout the country.

Later it was found that the majority of the deported immigrants had no connection whatever with any radical organizations. But at the time the mass arrests had the effect of making the American people and Congress more determined than ever to restrict immigration. By then even the owners of factories, railways, and mines, who had favored immigration in the past, sided with those who wanted to stop it or reduce it.

In February, 1921, Congress passed a bill that was designed to reduce the flood of immigration to a small trickle. President Wilson vetoed it, but when Warren G. Harding succeeded him in the White House a few months later, the bill became law. By approving the law, Harding became the first American President to say no to the words of the poet Emma Lazarus which appear on the base of the Statue of Liberty:

> Give me your tired, your poor,
> Your huddled masses yearning to breathe free,
> The wretched refuse of your teeming shore.
> Send these, the homeless, tempest-tossed to me:
> I lift my lamp beside the golden door!

The Immigration Law of 1921 made a mockery of these lines. It stipulated that only 3 percent of all the immigrants who were here in 1910 could be admitted into the country annually. And it established the system of selecting immigrants by quota, according to the countries of their origin. Like the literacy test, it pointedly discriminated against immigration from Europe's Southern and Eastern countries.

But the enemies of immigration were not yet satisfied. Now that the "golden door" to the nation had been partly shut, they were eager to shut it as far as they could. Three years later Congress passed the Immigration Act of 1924, which all but slammed the door shut and made it clearer than ever that non-Anglo-Saxon people, like the Italians, were not wanted here. The new legislation made two basic changes in the 1921 law: It reduced the quota percentage from 3 to 2 percent, and the 1890 census (when comparatively few Italians were in the United States), instead of the 1910 census, became the basis for determing how many immigrants would be admitted from each country each year.

The 1924 act cut down the total annual number of immigrants who could enter from 357,808 as specified in the 1921 law, to 164,ʿ 7. The new law reduced the quota of Italian immigrants to 3,845 per year. Northern countries, such as Germany, Great Britain, and Scandinavia, came out best. The German quota was the highest of all, with 51,227.

Not all Americans were happy about the new law. The bill had been eloquently opposed in both the House of Representatives and the Senate. Congressman Emanuel Celler attacked the idea of "Nordic supremacy," which was at the heart of the legislation. He quoted several leading experts to the effect that there is no such thing as a superior race, that all peoples are the products of their economic conditions, their education, and their habits.

In the Senate, David Walsh criticized those who called Southern European immigrants "mongrels, garbage, and riffraff" and cited labor statistics to show that they were among those who were doing a large percentage of the nation's work. Senator Magnus Johnson added that immigrants from Southern and Eastern Europe had undertaken many dangerous and unhealthful jobs that no one else was willing to do. He described a recent mining disaster in his home state of Minnesota which had killed forty men, most of them Southern Europeans.

But the majority of their colleagues in Congress were

in no mood to listen to such arguments. The general opinion was that the nation would be better off if it remained mainly Anglo-Saxon and Protestant. The Congress was still convinced that aliens who were not Anglo-Saxons often spread un-American radical ideas that were a threat to our form of government.

Part of this attitude grew out of one of the most publicized trials in American history–that of two Italian anarchists who were accused of murdering a paymaster and a guard at South Braintree, Massachusetts. The accused were Nicola Sacco, a fish peddler, and Bartolomeo Vanzetti, a shoemaker. They denied having any part in the murder. Their trial was considered unfair, and later much of the evidence against them was discredited. Yet they were denied a new trial and sentenced to die. The verdict aroused intense indignation in all parts of the world. Scores of leading intellectuals, in the United States and elsewhere, protested that the men were being sent to their death not because they were guilty but because they were radicals and foreigners.

The case dragged on for seven years, but despite the dedicated efforts of many liberals to have the verdict changed, the two men were finally executed. In a last and moving statement before the Court, Vanzetti, who had learned some English in jail while his case was being appealed, said: "I am suffering because I was a radical and indeed I am a radical. I have suffered because I was an Italian, and indeed I am an Italian."

Considering how large the Italian population in America had become, the number of radicals among them was surprisingly small. One of them was Arturo Giovannitti, the poet who had been one of the labor leaders in the 1912 Lawrence textile strike. He had come to the United States as a boy of sixteen and had worked as a coal miner and ditchdigger. But often he had been without work for long periods of time and had known the most painful kind of poverty. Becoming a Socialist, he had been an active champion of the poor and a bitter foe of capitalism, on which he blamed most of society's evils.

The best known of the Italian-American radicals was Carlo Tresca, the dynamic publisher of a New York newspaper issued in Italian, *Il Martello* (The Hammer). When Italy succumbed to the Fascist dictatorship of Benito Mussolini, Tresca began to devote most of his efforts to fighting Fascist propaganda in America. His weapons were his newspaper, his talent as an orator, and his big fists. In the thirties, when Mussolini was at the height of his power, Tresca and his friends broke up many a meeting of Fascist sympathizers in New York City. Calling himself an anarchist, he belonged to no political party, but his sympathies were always clearly on the side of people who were being exploited.

On a wintry evening in January, 1943, Tresca was shot in the back by an unknown assassin. Some believed he was murdered by one of Mussolini's hired gunmen. Others believed he was the victim of the Italian-American Fascist sympathizers he had attacked in his newspaper. There were also those who claimed he was killed by an agent of the Communists.

The rise of Fascism in Italy created a sharp difference of opinion among the Italians in America. There were many who sympathized with Mussolini's aims and applauded his victories, not because they were Fascists or understood the meaning of Fascism, but because they were proud to observe that under Mussolini's leadership their mother country was commanding the attention of the world. They saw no evil in Fascism. Neither did a number of leading American newspapers, which kept praising Mussolini for bringing more efficiency to Italy, especially in making the trains run on time. Nor did the leaders of the Italian-American community, who openly admired Mussolini and received decorations from him for their support.

But there were also Italian Americans who understood the horrors of Fascism and tried to enlighten their countrymen. Men like Tresca, Giovannitti, Luigi Antonini, and Girolomo Valente (the editor of the Socialist newspaper *La Stampa Libera*) led the fight against Italian Fascism. But their influence did not extend far beyond New York City. The Italian daily newspaper *Il Progresso,* which supported Mussolini, had many thousands of readers and was far more influential.

In New York there were a number of open clashes between the Italian sympathizers of Fascism and its opponents. One of them took place on Memorial Day, in 1927, while the Fascists and the anti-Fascists were conducting their annual parades. Violent fighting broke out between the two groups, and two of the black-shirted Fascists were killed. When two of the anti-Fascists were charged with the murders, they were defended by the celebrated civil liberties lawyer Clarence Darrow and acquitted. There were also instances when Fascists smashed the presses of anti-Fascist newspapers. In retaliation, the presses of Fascist publications were smashed by anti-Fascists.

When Mussolini declared war on Ethiopia in 1935, his supporters in the United States stepped up their propaganda efforts in his behalf. As a result, many Italian-American women donated their marriage rings to the Fascist government to help pay for the war. In some Little Italys, such as the one in Cleveland, the hope of an Italian victory was so keen that when the Fascist armies captured the capital of Ethiopia, there was a public celebration.

All this changed as soon as Mussolini became an ally of Adolf Hitler, the Nazi dictator of Germany. As far as most Italian Americans were concerned, the Italian dictator had now revealed his true colors as a reckless and egomaniacal figure who would bring more sorrow than glory to Italy. Those who had been for him in the past began to realize that their feelings had been based on their nostalgic love for Italy rather than on any real knowledge of Fascism. To make their loyalty to the United States government better known, a good many Italian immigrants applied for American citizenship that year.

But thousands of other Italians remained aliens, some because their inability to cope with the English language disqualified them for citizenship; others because they had lived in Little Italys for many years, more or less removed from the "American" world, and did not fully appreciate the value of citizenship. In 1940, when the American government registered and fingerprinted all German, Italian, and Japanese immigrants who were not citizens, it was found that the Italian alien group was the largest of all —approximately 650,000.

Yet when the Justice Department arrested all the aliens who were considered dangerous to the wartime security of the nation, fewer than 200 Italians were taken into custody and interned. During a tour of internment camps shortly after the United States entered World War II, I spoke with a number of the Italian internees, trying to find out why they had been arrested. One of them told me it was because of a letter he wrote to the President of the United States a few months before the United States declared war on Italy. "I told him that I was against such a war because I considered Italy my mother and America my father and I didn't want to see them fighting with one another."

Another had been arrested for belonging to an Italian-American Fascist organization. He said he had joined the organization because he thought that the stronger Fascism became, the more respect there would be for the Italian immigrants in America. He also told me that he had a son who had enlisted in the American Army and was fighting in Italy. Some months later I learned that the son had been killed in action and that the father had then been released from the internment camp.

Unlike their parents, the children of Italian immigrants showed little interest in the rise of Italian Fascism. Being thoroughly involved in the American life around them, they felt no sentimental bond with Italy. Yet their problems of adjustment were often more painful than those of their parents. Most of all, they wanted to be considered Americans. But as children they had been obliged to live two lives: to be Italians at home, where their parents often spoke nothing but Italian and lived as though they were still in Italy, and to be Americans with their playmates and at school. Because children usually like to be like other children and don't want to be thought of as different, the children of the immigrants were often embarrassed by their parents' foreign ways.

In his autobiography Fiorello H. LaGuardia remembers how he experienced this kind of embarrassment when he was a boy of ten growing up in Prescott, Arizona. An organ-grinder with a monkey had come to town, and his American playmates began to tease young Fiorello. "A dago with a monkey," they cried. "Hey, Fiorello, you're a dago too. Where's your monkey?" Young Fiorello felt even more hurt and ashamed when his father came along and began speaking to the organ-grinder in Italian and even invited him home for a macaroni meal.

Years later, when LaGuardia became New York's mayor, one of his first acts was to ban all organ-grinders from the streets of New York. His official reason was that they interfered with traffic safety, but in his heart he wondered whether it was because of the organ-grinder who had caused him so much hurt and embarrassment when he was a boy in Arizona.

When the sons and daughters of Italian immigrants became adults, they were more anxious than ever to be considered full-fledged Americans. But sometimes they found themselves rebuffed by other Americans, particularly by those employers who steadfastly refused to hire anyone of Italian origin. To avoid being rejected, some

Italian Americans changed their names. One of my relatives who had trained to be a schoolteacher, discovered that her Italian name prevented her from getting a position in the upstate New York area where she lived. As soon as she changed her name to Adams, she was hired. Many other sons and daughters of immigrants changed their names simply because their Italian names were too difficult to spell.

World War II had a revolutionary effect on the relationship between Italian Americans and the rest of the American world. By the time the war was over the major prejudices against them had all but crumbled. On the domestic front the same employers who had formerly refused to employ men and women of Italian origin had been compelled by the general labor shortage to employ persons of all nationality groups. They soon discovered, of course, that their Italian-American workers were as reliable and proficient as the best of their employees. Throughout the war, in every field of endeavor, Italian Americans and other Americans worked more closely together. As the gap between them narrowed, they learned to trust one another as they never had in the past.

On the military front the sons of Italian immigrants proved that they were willing to fight and die for the United States. About 500,000 Italian Americans served in the armed forces. Many were killed or wounded, some while fighting the Germans in Italy. Those who saw action in Italy often were valuable emissaries for the American Army since they could speak to the Italians in their own language.

At least a dozen Italian-American soldiers received

Congressional Medals of Honor. One was Marine Sergeant John Basilone of New Jersey, who for three days battled an entire Japanese regiment in Guadalcanal, with no other assistance than his machine gun. General Douglas MacArthur called him "a one man army." Later in the war Sergeant Basilone was killed while the Marines were landing at Iwo Jima. The Navy named a destroyer in his honor. Another Navy destroyer was named after Army Corporal Anthony Damato of Pennsylvania, one of two Italian-American brothers killed in action.

The United States history of World War II is studded with the daring deeds of soldiers who were the sons of Italian immigrants. One of the war's greatest air aces was Captain Don Gentile, who shot down thirty Nazi planes. Another was Major A. Martini, who downed twenty-two Nazi planes in the Paris skies during a fifteen-minute battle.

In the years following the war an increasing number of Italian Americans entered the political arena on local, state, and national levels. And the integration of the Italians into the American community neared completion. By that time the grandchildren of Italian immigrants were becoming old enough to reap all the benefits of being full-fledged Americans.

7

The Contributions They Made

THE EVIDENCE of how the Italians helped build America is still around us: subways, skyscrapers, aqueducts, railroads, canals, roads, reservoirs, dams. But a more lasting contribution has been their impact on the personality of America. Actually, there has been an exchange of influences. America has influenced the Italian immigrants with its youth and vigor, while the Italians have sown throughout the nation the seeds of their warmth and wisdom.

As the descendants of an ancient culture, the Italians brought with them their talent for the art of living and shared it freely with the country of their adoption. Poor though they were in material goods, they have always been rich in their love of people, in their appreciation for the goodness of food, and in their celebration of family life. All these Mediterranean qualities have enhanced the nation's personality.

Part of the Italian immigrants' contribution to the American art of living was made through the delicious native dishes they prepared in their kitchens. Their cooking became popular with Americans almost from the time they began to arrive. Early in the century Italian restaurants sprang up everywhere, often with Neapolitan chefs in charge, and soon spaghetti became widely accepted as a standard American dish. In more recent years, pizza has become another great favorite with Americans. It is believed that more pizza is now eaten in the United States than in Italy.

The Italians also acquainted Americans with *caffe espresso,* as well as their own kinds of ice cream, *spumone* and *biscotto tortone.*They also taught us many ways of adding to the flavor of food, with such herbs as oregano and basil and with garlic. At one time, my mother recalled, Americans sharply critized Italian immigrants for smelling of garlic. The complaint is seldom heard any longer for the simple reason that Americans now use garlic in their cooking almost as often as Italians.

The Italians made Americans aware of many foods they had never known. Mussels was one of them. Before the Italians began arriving, these shiny black-shelled creatures that cling to rocks and piers were generally ignored. Now they are regarded as a fine seafood delicacy. The Italians also introduced to many Americans such vegetables as broccoli, zucchini, escarole, endive, cardoon, chicory, dandelion. To the vineyards of California the immigrants brought a variety of Italian grapes, which produce several Mediterranean types of wines that are popular throughout America.

Even while the Italians were adding to the pleasures of eating, they were also nourishing the soul of America with their superb music and musicians. With the possible exception of the Negroes, no other people have contributed as much to this important aspect of the nation's culture. Perhaps the greatest opera singer in history was Neapolitian-born Enrico Caruso, who was the Metropolitan Opera Company's leading tenor from 1903 until his death in 1920. Another world-famous Italian musician was the eminent conductor Arturo Toscanini, who left Fascist Italy in 1926 in protest against Mussolini's regime and led the New York Philharmonic from then until 1937. After that he conducted the NBC Symphony Orchestra in a long series of radio concerts that helped popularize classical music in the United States. Toscanini retired in 1952 at the age of eighty-seven, after repeatedly being hailed by music critics as the greatest conductor of the century.

To those two names can be added scores of other renowned Italian musicians, mainly singers, who thrilled American audiences in all of the nation's large cities. One of the most acclaimed was the great Adelina Patti. Some others include Ezio Pinza, the basso who after a long career in Italian opera became the star of the big hit American musical *South Pacific;* Giovanni Martinelli, Beniamino Gigli, Renata Tebaldi, Pasquale Amato, Giuseppe de Luca, Lucrezia Bori, Giacomo Lauri-Volpe, Luisa Tetrazzini, Cesare Siepi, Licia Albanese, Amelita Galli-Curci. In the field of opera composition the Italian-born Gian-Carlo Menotti has written many works for the American musical scene. His short opera *Amahl and the Night Visitors* has often been performed on nationwide television.

The daughters and sons of Italian immigrants have also played a prominent role in the nation's musical world. Among them are the composers Vincent Persichetti, Peter Mennin and his brother·Louis Mennini, Walter Piston, Paul Creston, and Norman Dello Joio and the singers Rosa and Carmela Ponselle, Vivian Della Chiesa, Marguerite Piazza, Anna Moffo, and Richard Bonelli.

No other nationality group has produced more performers of popular music. Frank Sinatra, Perry Como, Dean Martin, Frankie Laine, Tony Bennett, Vic Damone, Constance Fanconero (better known as Connie Frances), and Joni James have been among the most popular of the popular song vocalists. There have also been many bandleaders, including such familiar personalities as Guy Lombardo, Carmen Cavallaro, Henry Mancini, Frankie Carle, Louis Prima.

In the early years of jazz some of its outstanding pioneer performers were Italian Americans. Dominick James LaRocca, a member of the Original Dixieland Band, is said to have strongly influenced the art of Bix Beiderbecke, perhaps the most lauded cornet player in American jazz. The violinist Leon Rappallo, the son of a Sicilian immigrant, was one of the famous New Orleans Rhythm Kings. Wingy Manone and Joe Marsala were among the notable jazzmen of the thirties.

An Italian-American musician who became one of the nation's most effective labor leaders was James Caesar

Petrillo of Chicago. He successfully persuaded thousands of American musicians that they could get better wages and steadier employment by joining a union. For many years he was national president of the powerful American Federation of Musicians.

Many an Italian American has charmed millions of Americans through the medium of the stage and motion pictures. On the silent screen no star enjoyed a more ardent following than Rudolph Valentino. More recent performers have included Mario Lanza, Sal Mineo, Jimmy Durante, Lou Costello, Jimmy Savo, Ernest Borgnine, Don Ameche, Rosanno Brazzi, Piere Angeli, Ben Gazzara, Anna Maria Alberghetti, and Anna Maria Italiano, better known by her stage name Anne Bancroft. There have also been brilliant Italian-American directors, among them Vincente Minnelli and Frank Capra. Some of the most delightful comedies to come out of Hollywood were directed by this Sicilian-born immigrant.

The American sports world, which has always been a boon to young athletes who cannot afford to stay in school for long, naturally attracted thousands of Italian Americans. They entered every field of sport, and a great number of them became champions, especially as baseball and football players and in the ring.

The most famous of all the baseball players was Joe DiMaggio, "the greatest Yankee of them all," whose uniform is in the Baseball Hall of Fame. He and a number of other Italian-American players helped the New York Yankees maintain their world championship for a record-breaking span of time. Yogi Berra, Phil Rizzuto, Tony Lazzeri, Frank Crosetti, Vic Raschi were among them.

More recently Joe Pepitone has been an outstanding Yankee. Italian-American major-league baseball stars have also included Harry "Cookie" Lavagetto, Carl Furillo, Dolf Camilli, Al Gionfriddo, Frank Malzone, Dominick and Vince DiMaggio (brothers of the immortal Joe), and others.

The sons of Italian immigrants have also scored high in college and professional football, both as players and as coaches. One of the most successful football coaches in college history was Lou Little of Columbia University, whose original name, Piccolo, means "little." In professional football few coaches have been more expert or more admired than Vince Lombardi.

Numerous championships have been won by Italian Americans in the boxing world. Rocky Marciano held the world's heavyweight boxing title to the day of his retirement from the ring. Tony Canzoneri won three different boxing titles: He was featherweight, junior lightweight, and lightweight champion. Italian-American titleholders have included among others the brothers Joe and Vince Dundee, Tony DeMarco, Fidel LaBarba (winner of the world flyweight title in the Olympics), Petey Scalzo, Rocky Graziano, and Peter Gulotta, who fought under the name of Pete Herman.

As one might expect of a people who have produced many of the world's greatest artists, Italian Americans began contributing to the development of American art almost from the time they first arrived here. In Italy Constantino Brumidi had distinguished himself with the frescoes he painted in the Vatican. When he came here in 1848 as a political exile, he was commissioned to do a series of frescoes in the Capitol at Washington based on dramatic episodes in American history. The artist, who signed one of the larger frescoes "C. Brumidi, Artist, Citizen of the U.S.," soon became known as the Michaelangelo of the Capitol.

Another Italian refugee, Count Luigi Palma di Cesnola, who received the Congressional Medal of Honor for his bravery as a colonel in the American Civil War, was appointed the first director of the Metropolitan Museum of Art in 1879. He held that position until his death a quarter of a century later and was credited with having established the Metropolitan as one of the most important museums in the world.

An Italian family of six sculptors—Attilio Piccirilli and his five brothers—were commissioned to do several monuments shortly after their arrival in the United States in 1888. Their memorial for the soldiers and sailors who lost their lives on the battleship *Maine* during the Spanish-American War stands in New York's Central Park. New York has a number of monuments and war memorials by other Italian-American sculptors. One of them is the life-size figure of Giuseppe Verdi, the most beloved of the Italian opera composers, which shows him with some of the opera characters he created. The monument, by Pasquale Civiletti, dominates New York's Verdi Square.

More recent Italian-American sculptors of note have included Beniamino Bufano, whose monuments of stainless steel in San Francisco add to the beauty of that city; Harry Bertoia, who became a noted designer of furniture, as well as a sculptor; Vincent Riu, a former marble cutter whose abstract sculpture is widely admired for its lyric quality; Conrad Marca-Relli, who is both a sculptor and a painter; and Ezio Martinelli.

Italian-American painters have long been in the forefront of modern art. They include Joseph Stella, who pioneered in American Cubist painting; Louis Guglielmi, whose paintings are in many museums; Gregorio Prestopino, whose renditions of life in Harlem became the subject of a fascinating motion-picture short; and the brothers Salvatore, Angelo, and Biagio Pinto. In addition, there are Frank Stella, Joseph De Martini, Paul Pollaro, Jean Liberte, Nicholas Marsicano, Laurence Calcagno, Angelo Savelli, Peppino Mangravite, Attilio Salemmi, and many others.

One of the nation's leading craftsmen in the ancient art of stained glass and mosaics is Nicola D'Ascenzo. Examples of his exquisite work are in the Washington Memorial Chapel at Valley Forge, the Princeton University Chapel, the Folger Library in Washington, D.C., and the Cathedral of St. John the Divine in New York City.

Modern science, which is said to have begun with the discoveries of Galileo Galilei in Italy more than 400 years ago, has been advanced by a number of Italian-American scientists. One of the most important scientists of the century was Enrico Fermi, who came to the United States as a refugee from Fascist Italy in 1939. Under the auspices of the American government, in 1942 he directed the research in nuclear physics that resulted in the first atom bomb. A Nobel Prize winner, Fermi is generally given credit for opening the door to the atomic age. To express its gratitude to this brilliant scientist, the American government awarded him the highest honor that can be bestowed on a civilian, the Medal of Merit.

Other Italian scientists who came to the United States during the same period were Bruno Rossi, whose work in cosmic rays is internationally renowned; Dr. Emilio Segre, who won the Nobel Prize in Physics in 1959 for his work in the structure of matter; Dr. Eugene G. Fubini, who was a member of Enrico Fermi's nuclear research team and later became Assistant Secretary of Defense.

Altogether there were five Italian-American scientists besides Fermi who participated in the research for the atomic bomb. Several of them have since served on the Atomic Energy Commission, which controls the development of atomic power for peacetime as well as wartime uses. Dozens of other Italian-American scientists have worked in government agencies dealing with agriculture, in public health, and in the Bureau of Standards. Many others have been associated with private industry and with many universities and colleges.

Among the first Italian-American scientists to win world fame was Giuseppe Bellanca, who came here in 1911 after being a pioneer in Italian aviation. In 1922 he designed and built the first five-seater cabin monoplane in the United States. This airplane ultimately won first prizes in thirteen events. Later Bellanca also designed the first monoplanes to cross both the Atlantic and the Pacific. Another Italian aviation pioneer who contributed to the development of American aviation was Enea Bossi. In 1922 he designed the first all-welded stainless-steel airplane and in 1937 a plane that established a new world record for sustained flight.

In the field of letters a fascinating body of literature

has been produced by Italian-American novelists who have described the life of the immigrants and shown how they reacted to the strange American world around them during the years when they felt most uprooted. Some of the best of these writers have included Pietro Di Donato (who was a bricklayer, like his father, before he became an author), John Fante, Jo Pagano, Guido D'Agostino, Michael and Raymond De Capite, George Panetta, Diana Cavallo, Mario Puzo, Octavia Waldo, and Lucius Longo. Although their novels have a great deal of literary merit, relatively few Americans have read them. The sole exception is Di Donato's *Christ in Concrete,* which was widely distributed because it was a book club selection.

Di Donato's work also includes a book of nonfiction: *Mother Cabrini: Immigrant Saint,* the story of an Italian-American nun who was elevated to sainthood for her work in American slums. One of the most distinguished of all the Italian-American nonfiction writers has been Frances Winwar (the last name is a translation of her original name, Vinciguerra), whose most impressive books have dealt with prominent figures in English literature.

More successful than the novelists in attracting attention have been the Italian-American poets. One of the first to win acclaim was Arturo Giovannitti, whose collected poems *Arrows in the Gale* includes the powerful work "The Walker," written while he was in jail during the Lawrence textile strike. The Italian-born poet Emanuel Carnevali made a deep impression on the American literary scene during the twenties. The struggle of the immigrant was one of his themes, and in one poem he wrote:

America, you gather the hungry people
And give them new hungers for the old ones.

In more recent years Lawrence Ferlinghetti, author of the popular *Coney Island of the Mind,* has become one of the most widely read poets of his generation. Other prominent poets of Italian origin include John Ciardi, the poetry editor of the *Saturday Review,* whose books have won him many honors; Henry Rago, the editor of *Poetry;* and Gregory Corso.

Of the new hungers that the immigrants developed in America, that of educating their sons was perhaps the strongest. This was especially true among families where the parents had acquired some education, however little, in Italy. Despite their general poverty, thousands of their American-born sons were trained to enter the medical, legal, and teaching professions.

Italian-American doctors have contributed immeasurably to the health of the nation as general practitioners, specialists, surgeons, professors of medicine, and administrative heads of hospitals. In the field of education, more and more Italian Americans have become teachers and chief administrative officers in grade schools, secondary schools, colleges, and universities. As long ago as 1945 more than 10,000 Italian Americans were teaching in the New York City public school system alone.

The sons of Italian immigrants have shown a special aptitude for the legal profession and have excelled in every branch of it. It has even included some daughters of immigrants, notably Lisa Aversa Richette, who for ten years headed the children's court in Philadelphia as assistant district attorney. At present there are more than 450 judges of Italian origin officiating in our courts. One of them, the late Michael A. Musmanno, a Supreme Court Justice of Pennsylvania, achieved international prominence after World War II as one of the judges of the War Crimes Tribunal in Nuremberg. Judge Musmanno, an ardent champion of Christopher Columbus' exploits, died on Columbus Day, 1968.

Although it was not until the early thirties that Italian-American lawyers began entering the political arena in considerable numbers, they have become a basic part of the nation's power structure and won recognition of the Italian-American community as a political force. There have been at least eight governors of Italian origin, more than thirty Representatives in the United States Congress, two Cabinet members, one Senator, and many other important federal and state officials.

The Senator is John Pastore of Rhode Island, who formerly served as governor of that state. The first Italian-American Cabinet member was Anthony J. Celebrezze, Secretary of Health, Education, and Welfare in the Kennedy and Johnson administrations. The second Cabinet member, appointed by President Nixon as Secretary of Transportation, is John A. Volpe, former governor of Massachusetts.

The Johnson administration also included two Presidential assistants of Italian lineage, Joseph A. Califano, Jr., and Jack Valenti, the present commissioner of the Motion Picture industry. During the Truman administration the United States Commissioner of Immigration and Naturalization was Ugo Carusi, the son of an immigrant quarry worker from Carrara. The nation's first Italian-American Commissioner of Immigration was Edward Corsi, an immigrant born near Naples. Appointed by President Herbert Hoover, he held that position for twelve years.

A remarkably large number of Italian Americans have been elected American mayors of big and small communities, including Buffalo and Rochester, New York; Newark, New Jersey; New York City, New Orleans, and San Francisco. Robert S. Maestri served as mayor of New Orleans for a full decade, from 1936 to 1946. Angelo Rossi was San Francisco's mayor for an even longer time, from 1931 to 1946. The present mayor of that city is also an Italian American, Joseph Alioto, who nominated Hubert H. Humphrey for the Presidency at the 1968 Democratic National Convention.

In 1950 all three of the chief contenders for the office of mayor of New York City were Italian Americans: Edward Corsi, Judge Ferdinand Pecora, and Vincent Impelliteri. Impelliteri, who won the election, made a pilgrimage shortly afterward to the Sicilian village where his father was born. Perhaps the most esteemed of all New York mayors was the vigorous Italian American Fiorello H. LaGuardia, who could speak five languages.

Affectionately known as the Little Flower (the English translation for Fiorello), LaGuardia, a progressive, was elected mayor three consecutive times, after having served in Congress for fourteen years. When he died in 1947, he was mourned by Americans in every part of the nation. His courage, honesty, and genuine concern for the poor had won him a far-flung reputation as a model public servant. One of the Little Flower's most endearing traits was his ability to be himself at all times. Long after he died, New Yorkers still remembered how, during a long newspaper strike, he read the most popular of the daily comic strips over the radio so that the children of New York would not miss out on what was happening to their favorite characters.

From the earliest days of Italian immigration there have been prosperous Italian-American businessmen, especially in the field of banking. Bankers began to flourish as soon as the immigrants needed their services to save money or borrow it. Not speaking English, they preferred to deal with Italian-American bankers who knew their language. Some of the early bankers were not always honest, and many an immigrant lost all his hard-earned savings. Those who could be trusted, however, often became increasingly wealthy as more and more immigrants became active in the American economy.

The most successful of all the bankers was the financial genius Amadeo Pietro Giannini, the father of the Bank of America, which grew into the world's largest banking institution. The son of an immigrant from Genoa, Giannini began working for a San Francisco produce firm at the age of twelve and had become a partner in the business by the time he was nineteen. In 1906, when San Francisco was all but destroyed by an earthquake and fire, he went into the banking business. Using the most direct techniques possible to get clients, he loaded a wagon with money and went out among the ruins of the city to make loans to people who needed to rebuild their stores and homes.

Within a few months Giannini's Bank of Italy as he had called the small store he first rented as an office, had branches in all parts of California where Italians needed to borrow money for their farms, vineyards, and business establishments. A shrewd judge of character, he often trusted people who owned little or nothing. "Your face is enough security for me," he would say to them, and lend them the money they needed.

There have been thousands of other Italian Americans not mentioned in this chapter who have made individual contributions to the economy and culture of the nation. But the greatest contribution was made by the mass of Italian immigrants who never achieved fame, wealth, or prestige. Their success came from helping build the country, bringing up their American-born children, and gradually losing their feeling of being uprooted. Over the years they were able to prove to themselves and to everyone else that here is where they belonged.

8

America Is Also Italian

OUR AMERICAN cities still have their Little Italys, but
they are no longer considered separate from the rest of
the community. The hostility is gone. The barriers between Italians and non-Italians are down, and there has
been more and more intermarriage between the children
of Italians and those of other nationality groups. By now
it has become clear that the fabric of our country is
closely interwoven with the hopes and achievements of
the 5,000,000 men and women who came here from
Italy. Their population legacy is impressive: 22,000,000
Americans of Italian origin—about 10 percent of the
total population.

Through the years the older American groups have
gained in their appreciation of the Italians and the other
immigrants of this century. Instead of criticizing them

for being different, as they once did, they accept them with all their differences. They are more aware than ever that Walt Whitman's phrase "a nation of nations" is a true description of our country, where people of all national origins can live and work together as long as they share a common faith in freedom and democracy.

It has taken time for this awareness to spread. As recently as 1952 Congress passed an immigration law that continued the policy of discriminating against people who were not of Anglo-Saxon origin. President Truman vetoed the law because, in his own words, it was based on the idea that "Americans with English or Irish names were better people and better citizens than Americans with Greek or Polish names." Despite President Truman's veto, the Immigration and Naturalization Act of 1952 became law.

During his term of office President John F. Kennedy, the great-grandson of an Irish immigrant, also objected to the act of 1952. He urged Congress to pass a new immigration law that would remove all suggestions of nationality discrimination. Only with such a law, he said, could we "turn to the world, and to our past, with clean hands and a clear conscience." He proposed scrapping the quota system of selecting immigrants according to their country of origin, using, instead, a new method of selection that would be based on equality and fair play for the peoples of all nations.

Two years after his assassination the legislation recommended by President Kennedy became law. Called the Immigration Act of 1965 and signed by President Lyndon B. Johnson, it stipulated that, starting on July 1,

1968, immigrants from all countries would be admitted chiefly on the basis of their work skills and on any close relationships they might have to immigrants already here. No longer would the country in which an immigrant was born be taken into consideration.

Although the new law did not open the "golden door" any wider, it represented a clear-cut victory for all American immigrants from countries that had been discriminated against since 1921. Above all, the change in immigration policy was a moral victory for the whole nation since it could now face itself and the rest of the world with a clearer conscience.

As the largest immigrant group of this century, the Italian Americans undoubtedly influenced the passage of the new law by the fine record they had established as loyal and useful members of our society. Nowadays they enjoy a greater degree of popularity than they have ever known. Yet there are still occasional echoes of the anti-Italian prejudice that once plagued them. It is usually found in magazine fiction, comic strips, and, to a lessening extent, on television and motion-picture screens. Careless writers of popular fiction and comic strips too often give Italian names to their villains. And articles in newspapers and magazines too often use the terms "Mafia" and "Cosa Nostra" simply for their sensational value, without regard to accuracy.

Both practices give the unfair impression that the Italian Americans include a good many criminals. Actually, the opposite is true. Statistics show that our 22,000,000 Italian Americans have one of the lowest crime rates of any nationality group in the nation.

The problem of racial prejudice remains one of America's most serious troubles. Although it is no longer directed at the Italians and the other early-century immigrants, it continues to be widespread and destructive. Its chief victims nowadays are the American Negroes and the Puerto Ricans, who began arriving in large numbers in the mid-forties to escape the poverty of their island. The history of discrimination against the Negroes is a long and tragic one that can be resolved only by making sure that the Negroes are given all the rights and opportunities that other Americans have. The story of the Puerto Rican Americans is a shorter one, but they have suffered from exactly the same kind of hostility that the Italian immigrants knew for many years.

Sadly enough, some of the Americans who are most guilty of prejudice against the Negroes and Puerto Ricans are the sons and daughters of the very immigrants who were once the victims of discrimination.

Fortunately, the great majority of Americans believe in equality for everyone and realize that prejudice is a cancer that can disable the nation if it is not conquered in time. But more must come from that realization. It is not enough just to *believe* in equality. It is necessary to *practice* equality with Americans of all races and backgrounds. Only in that way can the words "democracy and freedom" truly mean what they should mean in the United States.

For Further Reading

GLAZER, NATHAN, and MOYNIHAN, DANIEL P., *Beyond the Melting Pot.* Cambridge, Mass, M.I.T. Press and Harvard University Press, 1963 (reprint edition).

HANDLIN, OSCAR, ed., *Children of the Uprooted.* New York, George Braziller, 1966.

HANDLIN, OSCAR, *The Uprooted.* New York, Grosset's Universal Library, 1951 (reprint edition).

HIGHAM, JOHN, *Strangers in the Land.* New York, Atheneum, 1963 (reprint edition).

KENNEDY, JOHN F., *A Nation of Immigrants.* Introduction by Robert F. Kennedy. New York, Harper Torchbook, 1964 (reprint edition).

MANGIONE, JERRE, *Mount Allegro.* Introduction by Dorothy Canfield. New York, Hill and Wang American Century Series, 1963 (reprint edition).

PISANI, LAWRENCE FRANK, *The Italian in America.* New York, Exposition Press, 1957.

WITTKE, CARL, *We Who Built America.* Cleveland, Press of Case Western Reserve, 1964 (reprint edition).

ZIEGLER, BENJAMIN MUNN, ed., *Immigration: An American Dilemma.* Boston, D.C. Heath Company's Problems in American Civilization series, 1953 (pamphlet).

Glossary

Biscotto tortone—An ice-cream dessert topped with chopped toasted almonds.

Briscola—An Italian card game in which the players are permitted to exchange signals with their partners.

Caffe espresso—Italian-styled black coffee served in small quantities.

Comare—A godmother or a woman who is a matron (or maid) of honor at a wedding.

Compare—A godfather, or a man who is the best man at a wedding.

Destino—Destiny, or fate.

Festa—A feast or a holiday.

Gabelloto—Manager or leaseholder of a large farm.

Padrone—A boss or employer.

Scopa—The word means "broom," but it is also the name of a popular Italian card game.

Spumone—A dessert that combines various flavors of ice cream and sherbet.

Stampa libera—The free press.

Stratto—A sun-dried tomato paste that is used in cooking macaroni sauce.

Index

INDEX

The Author

Jerre Mangione was born of Sicilian immigrant parents who came to Rochester, New York, shortly after the turn of the century. He grew up among scores of relatives in a household where only Sicilian was spoken. Mr. Mangione worked his way through Syracuse University and later became an editor for a New York book publisher. In the 1940's, he served for six years as special assistant to the U. S. Commissioner of Immigration and Naturalization. Mr. Mangione is now professor of English and head of the creative writing program at the University of Pennsylvania. He is the author of six books, three of which deal with Italians.

Mangione- America is also   c.1

M   Int

DATE DUE Italian

Jun 2 '70 A867			
Aug 27 '70 B9			

PRINTED IN U.S.A.